My American Flight to Egypt:

A Western Evangelical Discovers the Ancient Faith

My American Flight to Egypt:
A Western Evangelical Discovers the Ancient Faith

Thilo Irenaeus Young
with
Anastasia Young

AGORA
UNIVERSITY
PRESS
EST. 2012

Copyright © 2022 Agora University Press

All rights reserved. Printed in the United States of America. No part of this book may be used or reproduced in any manner whatsoever without written permission except in the case of brief quotations embodied in critical articles or reviews.

For more information, contact: aupress@agora.ac

Agora University Press: press.agora.ac

ISBN 978-1-950831-42-5 (print)
       978-1-950831-43-2 (e-book)

Printed in the United States of America

His Holiness **POPE TAWADROS II**
Pope and Patriarch of Alexandria and the See of St. Mark.

His Holiness **PATRIARCH IGNATIUS APHREM II**
Patriarch of Antioch and All the East.

Dedication

*With gratitude to my beloved Anastasia,
with whom I continue to journey,
Emmanuel, my dear friend, brother, godfather, and continuing guide,
Abouna Daniel, our friend, father, and guide into the Church,
Abouna Bishoy, my profound and steadfast friend and Father,
and Abouna Gregory, my devoted guide and Father of Confession.*

Table of Contents

Foreword……………………………………………………viii
Introduction…………………………………………………1

Part I: The Long Desert Journey

Chapter 1……………………………………………………..6
Chapter 2……………………………………………………20
Chapter 3……………………………………………………25
Chapter 4……………………………………………………31
Chapter 5……………………………………………………41
Chapter 6……………………………………………………53
Chapter 7……………………………………………………60

Part II: Anastasia's Story

Chapter 8……………………………………………………81
Chapter 9……………………………………………………87
Chapter 10…………………………………………………..91
Chapter 11…………………………………………………100
Chapter 12…………………………………………………102
Chapter 13…………………………………………………106
Chapter 14…………………………………………………110
Chapter 15…………………………………………………117
Chapter 16…………………………………………………119
Chapter 17…………………………………………………121
Chapter 18…………………………………………………129
Chapter 19…………………………………………………132

Part III: Settling In

Chapter 20…………………………………………………135
Chapter 21…………………………………………………138
Chapter 22…………………………………………………143
Chapter 23…………………………………………………162
Chapter 24…………………………………………………167

Chapter 25..185
Chapter 26..190
About the Authors..194

Foreword

In preaching after Eutropius had been taken captive, St. John Chrysostom taught, "When thou takest refuge in a Church, do not seek shelter merely in the place but in the spirit of the place. For the Church is not wall and roof but faith and life." The Coptic Orthodox Church is beautiful, filled with all the fullness of God. She is a mother and a harbor for those who sorrow or are in distress. She guards the deposit of faith and through the work of the Holy Spirit, she passes it on to her children throughout the generations. The Church has *spirit*, *faith*, and *life*, and Thilo and Anastasia were able to discover it.

Without getting into the academic nitty-gritty, they wrote a profound book of their journey, where one of the main "characters" is Coptic Orthodox practical theology. Their discovery of Orthodoxy—not just studying the faith but beginning to be formed by it—came by way of living in and experiencing the rhythmic interplay of *dogma* and *practice*. They experienced the theology of the Church, a theology as old as the words of Scripture, but older than the Bible.

Their joining the Coptic Orthodox Church was not the result of any wisdom on my part or of me "saying the right words." They had been searching all their lives for true living in communion with God through the Church. They yearned for the sacramental life. All of humanity does. I believe God ordained that I join them in this leg of their journey. I tried to guide them on their journey, taking them down a route I thought was safe and clear, but knowing it would take a long time, and I was committed to the journey. It was not easy, but God's grace was good to all of us. I offered them the vast ocean of the Church in which to swim, and I tried to be a lifeguard. At times, they almost drowned. At times, I almost drowned. Christ's merciful hand saved us all.

Their catechesis entailed two major components. One component was the classes, which included Bible Studies. During the span of over a year, on a weekly basis, we had purposeful conversations about the sources of our Orthodox theology and doctrine, our worship, the history of the Church and the development of the New Testament, of our Orthodox spirituality and practice. We spent time studying the Bible, especially St. Paul's Epistle to the Romans, a very important book for understanding "faith." The second component was our liturgical practice and worship. They needed to see and experience how Orthodox Christians worship and why they worshiped in this way. They needed to be shaped by the liturgical practices. They needed to feel fasting, and they needed to pray the psalms. They faithfully attended most services for over a year before they were baptized, and that included all-night Apocalypse Vigil and Divine Liturgy.

Let the reader note all the unnamed hands that participated in their journey and supported the service. The chanters who chanted, the quiet parishioners who venerated icons, those who smiled or welcomed them, the hands that cleaned the church and organized the books, and did so much more. The community played an integral role in this journey, and may they all be rewarded for their faithfulness and service.

Now as God used me to serve them, God also used them to serve me. When they appeared on the steps of the parish, I had some deep internal conflict about my own ministry. *Was I serving God as He wanted me to serve Him? If not, I wanted Him to change and guide me.* Admittedly, I was certainly not pleasing many parishioners, and I needed guidance from God—*was I wrong in my focus, or did I need to read the latest Protestant bestseller and try and baptize it for Orthodox consumption?* I was praying that God reassure me or that He show me the right direction for my ministry. Thilo and Anastasia became that reassurance for me.

May God continue to bless their spiritual journey, filling them with His love and peace, guiding them and us to the safe harbors of His Kingdom. I pray that this book be a support, help, and guide for all those who read. May God be glorified in and through this work. Glory to God in all things.

Fr. Daniel W. Habib

Mesori 6, 1738

August 12, 2022

INTRODUCTION

This is a recounting of personal experience, not a theological treatise. I suppose the primary audience I have in mind would likely be younger Copts, for whom I desire a deeper love and appreciation of what they have inherited and may take for granted. As I often say when I give talks, "I'm just holding up a mirror to show you who you are."

At the same time, I have found many older Copts at various times being interested in and appreciative of my views as being very much indicative of their own, only expressed in a way that they had sensed, but never really articulated, as well as enjoying the novelty of coming from an American. I suppose we all love to see others really appreciate and embrace the things we love. So, I can say that they are also in mind as I write.

For all Coptic Orthodox readers particularly, and all other Orthodox readers generally, who come from Orthodox homes (cradle Orthodox is the common phrase), I hope to also offer some understanding of why the faith they inherited is simply not harmonious with the perhaps appealing and likely dominant religion of those in this American culture who self-identify as Christians. There is no way around it. I think the American Evangelical beliefs and practices are wrong in many key areas, and disagreement is just plain offensive to many. I cannot avoid that. If I did not think they were fundamentally different, and that Orthodoxy was in fact right, I would have been a fool to convert and subject myself to the rigors of this church.

Also, I think of the Protestant/Evangelical inquirer, or would-be inquirer. To them I apologize in advance for any offense; that is not my intent. Yet, having come to a conclusion that these later Western schisms are not authentic representations of what the Apostles delivered to the churches, and not an unbroken continuity of that ancient faith, I will no doubt be found to be critical. I hope such a reader will bring to mind his own zeal for what he has determined to be true, as is (admirably) the case with so many Evangelicals as they engage in matters of truth with the unbelieving world around them.

Something which may well be noticed as being conspicuously absent is an affirmation of commonalities between the two religions. The scope of the writing being one of contrast, I'll only mention these here.

I have noticed an overwhelming majority of Copts from Egypt being aligned with American conservatism politically. I believe this is due primarily to a shared Bible which informs both their moral views and the traditional Christian American, both of which heavily emphasize one's own personal choices in moral conduct over and above past or present formative influences (systems) which may well have been and may still be major contributive factors. Indeed, as we all view the basics of the Biblical narrative, it begins with the Fall of Man. As we enter into our own phase of the story, we begin with an inheritance of fallenness which is not of our making or choosing. Nonetheless, the main thrust of the teachings is centered upon what to do in this situation—one of personal ownership and choices rather than a dwelling on influences beyond our immediate control (repentance)—as we go forward. The two, in their Biblical values regarding personal morality and faith (as opposed to approaches centering on general governmental systems as the issue of prime concern), dovetail rather seamlessly. For understandable reasons.

This is not to say that some of the younger, more liberal Copts are not informed by their Biblical values, but rather that the emphasis on one's personal responsibility and conduct is given a lesser place while the role of the system in distributing charity and equity is given a higher one. So, in this regard, there is a commonality between Copts and Protestants/Evangelicals on both sides of the political aisle. You will find no mention of politics in this writing; I only mention it here as it regards commonalities.

Also, in the area of love and acceptance, there is a shared common value, more so between younger Copts and Evangelicals. They see the warm and welcoming nature of the Evangelical western churches, in stark juxtaposition to the more enclosed culture of the older immigrant community, and in turn seek to foster that atmosphere in their parishes (I will go into the errors associated with a lack of awareness between the religious and the cultural as this well-intended endeavor plays out later in this writing).

There is the shared value of the teachings of Christ, although much less prevalent in many ways among Evangelicals than those of Saint Paul as they interpret him, regarding the salvific nature of those moral teachings. Nonetheless, the values do align.

And of course, there is the common value of benevolence, each sincerely believing theirs to be the more complete (at least) way to God.

I hope for sympathetic understanding when I use the terms "Protestant" or "Evangelical." Not seeking to parse out the numerous beliefs of the thousands of individual groups, I speak in more generalized terms. I would simply ask the reader, when he sees something which he believes does not really properly capture the beliefs of his particular group, to think of other groups of whom it is truer and simply say, "Okay, but this does not apply to me." Were we to sit down face to face and you try to explain why some point does not apply to your church, I would likely nod in agreement. Those in older forms of Protestantism will naturally find less of the criticisms of modern western Evangelicalism to be applicable to them.

I hasten to add that absolutely nothing you will read is an attack on the good people of the western faiths who often times pursue God and His truth with a zeal and honesty and dedication I would love to see mirrored among more of my Orthodox brothers and sisters. The criticisms are regarding beliefs and practices, not persons.

When I speak of Western or Protestant, I do not include Catholics or Anglicans, as a matter of clarification. My language is not intended to follow the pinpointed categories of a scholarly work. If one finds resonance within one's own tradition, okay. If not, okay. This is simply a personal narrative.

Lastly, nothing here being new to me regarding having discussed these matters with many other former Protestant/Evangelical converts to Orthodoxy, I am fairly certain that the reader or the inquirer from a common background as mine with one foot in the door of Orthodoxy will find much to resonate, and likely a few things of explanatory value to be obtained.

Thilo Young

Part I: The Long Desert Journey

Chapter 1

"By the guile of the serpent, we fell from eternal life…"
—Liturgy of Saint Basil

It's hard to know where to begin. So, I suppose I'll start at the beginning.

No. Wait. I need to go back further. Before that.

My mother was born in Westphalia, Germany in the summer of 1928 to what she conveyed to me as an abusive mother and a deeply moral, intelligent, and thoughtful father. Between the pre-World War II period of extreme German hardship and discord following the First World War and the punishing treaty of Versailles, and the rise of Hitler and ensuing war, hers was anything but a happy childhood. Early childhood photos, the few which remained, told the tale of a somber and serious Margarethe.

Both sides of her family being Marxist, as there weren't too many politically ideological options available, and having a rather idealistic and not overly realistic vision of the world, they became undesirables under the new Nazi regime. Her father spent the war in prison, likely saving his life, while she marched at the end of the Hitler Youth parades. The war ended when she was seventeen.

Although in my memories she was a very heavy-set woman, the emotional distress taking a toll in many ways including overeating, younger photos revealed a quite fetching younger lady. I dare even say gorgeous, although it feels funny to say that about *Omi* (German for "Grandma," a term which became her name to the family later in life).

Like clockwork, every April 20th she would proclaim, "It's that bastard's birthday!" She despised what he had done to her beloved Germany; she had a particular fondness and admiration for the Yiddish mamas of the Jews. In fact, she had a keen interest in all cultures and peoples, as well as being a rare romantic German. Similarly out of place, it seems she had an inquisitiveness and depth of sober insight which compelled her to ask the questions seldom heard from children her age.

Spending the war in Düsseldorf, an industrial city which was heavily bombed, and being claustrophobic, she told me stories of standing outside the air raid shelter, at the entrance, when the sirens rang and bombers flew over the city dropping their payloads, because she was afraid to go inside. She emotionally told the tale of having to go next door to warn her uncle, an epileptic, of the coming of the Gestapo to take him, prompting him to hang himself. She, and as she told me was also the case with most Germans, had no idea what happened in the camps until the war ended, being horrified at the news. Living in the midst of a war and just trying to eat and survive, with the camps being remote locations without visitors, this makes sense. Nonetheless, despite all this and many other regrettable stories of her experiences at the time, she also spoke of fondness regarding some aspects of life in Nazi Germany.

She told of a camaraderie among the youth, a strong sense of national pride in being a German, and displayed in her life a great embrace of the trained attributes she received: organization, accuracy, honor, hard work, and a staunch, steadfast, and unyielding demeanor.

Her housecleaning was legendary, being hired by a few people of more significant means to perform her "German cleaning" services in order to help supplement her meager income (as I was told, when her own mother went into labor with her, she was under an old stove with legs scrubbing the bottom and had to be pulled out). Mom would say, "These Americans make round corners when they clean. In Germany, the corners are square!" Never did she own a mop. It had to be done on hands and knees (her knees were blown out in later years from this work) in order to get to the edges. In her laundry, and I say this without exaggeration, you could take a square to check her linen closets and find them perfect. My shirts were folded without a single wrinkle in the same manner in which one would find them new in the package. These things were all part of a young girl's education in Germany, as well as cooking.

I remember a funny story reminiscing my mother's precision: if dinner was at 6:00 pm, the burners on the stove and oven would all be turned off simultaneously at 5:58 pm and the food placed on the table. She had a German rhyme for most things, and the one in this regard, translated into English, roughly said, "He who is late to dinner gets leftovers." After warning me, one day I arrived home for dinner at 6:03 pm. The doors were locked! I had to sit outside until everyone was done eating, then she let me in to eat from what remained. To this day, as my sister once put it, "I panic when I'm late for being early."

Good posture and proper speech were essential. She often spoke of the Prussians when discussing posture and told of the schools in Germany in which you were made to place a broom handle in front of your arms, and behind your back, for some extended period if you were caught slouching. Speech patterns and grammar told of one's social class.

I attribute any abilities I possess to see beyond black-and-white categories, as comforting and falsely grounding as embracing such a mindset may be, to her. Her experiences, conveying some good to be found in the worst of times and events, taught me to be mindful of the other side of any story. Things are seldom as simple as we would like to think.

I am reminded of another funny anecdote: we used to joke that one day we would be at her funeral, sobbing, and one of us would say "Mom's not with us no more", and she would sit up in her casket and say "*Any*more!" One day, as I recall it was about a year or two before her passing, I went to visit her with my then girlfriend (now wife, Anastasia) and found her in an unconscious state in which she had been for some days in the hospital. I leaned in toward her ear and said, "*Mach dein Augen offen*," meaning "open your eyes." To which she slowly opened them just a bit and replied, "*Mach DEINE Augen offen.*" Then closed them again for a couple more weeks. Anastasia, with a look of total confusion, asked "What just happened?!" To which I explained, "She just corrected my grammar."

Following the war, she moved to London to find work, where she met a Welshman and they married. The two immigrated to Canada then to the United States, where they eventually divorced after having two children.

Finding herself the mother of two, now living in El Monte, California (only locals know what that means, but I'll just say it wasn't exactly a desirable town), she met a handsome, muscular Latin man. In one aspect she was the most un-German: romanticism. She envisioned him as the dark, romantic type she had experienced in Europe, like the Greeks and Spaniards. And from what I gathered later in life she had been a bit of a wild woman. Well, this man was not quite the type of romantic Latin she had envisioned.

Jesse (Jesus) was the son of a former soldier who had ridden with Pancho Villa, who then turned bank robber and murderer before fleeing Mexico and taking on the first name of his two eldest brothers (it seems there was a custom of naming the first two sons after the father in case something happened to one, the other would carry on his name) to evade the law: Miguel Hernandez. Miguel had seventeen children (not all survived childbirth) with his much younger wife Victoria (my Nana) before dying in what I believe to have been a drunken accident involving a scaffold while most of his children were still young, my father Jesus being singled out as the black sheep (I remember my mother sarcastically joking with him about the irony of his name).

I recall a story being told about my father as a child working for a long period to save up money to buy a bicycle, only to have his mother take it and give it to one of the better boys. As told, this was typical of his childhood. His life was marked by drugs, alcohol, and crime. As I understood it, sometimes during colder winter months, he'd commit some small crime in order to be jailed in a warm cell with three square meals a day.

My mother was soon to discover this "romantic Latin" man was not what she had imagined, and his excellent muscular physical appearance was due to having just spent some years in the penitentiary lifting weights. I seem to recall the crime was smuggling illegal aliens into the country, but I'm not sure. Being in jail when I was born, as was his frequent residence, my mother gave me her surname (she and my dad never married), which was that of my brother and sister. This name from her first husband was not properly my identity, so I had it legally changed to the

English translation of her maiden name (Jung) when I turned eighteen. Not desiring to carry the name of my mostly absent father (while I did love him, he contributed little of positive value to my upbringing), but rather wanting something which drew from my mother and her heritage while at the same time embracing my very American identity, this name was my very personal choice of self-identity.

From the time of meeting my father, her story seems to take a dark turn. I have only one clear memory before adolescence, and when my sister, who remembers everything vividly, recounts some events (like the time they carried a dead body out of our home who had overdosed, or my favorite chair behind which I would hide when violence erupted, or the DEA raid), I consider myself fortunate not to remember. Better to let sleeping dogs lie.

My one vivid memory was my mother and I returning home to a dark house with a light on in the bathroom. I can't remember my age at the time, but it was the home where we lived when I was a child. As we moved through the living room and towards the light and open door, I could see my father slumped down on the floor, leaning against the wall, unconscious, a couple of his friends with him being surprised by our arrival, and needles and blood on the bathroom counter. My mother erupted in screams (let me tell you, that woman was a world class screamer!) and as they dragged him out, cupping their hands under his arms, his shoe caught on the door jamb and came off.

As you may have guessed, I grew up poor and our family was on welfare. I suppose this home was beyond dysfunctional, and thankfully I suppose my dad was frequently gone for extended periods. At least that's how it appears in retrospect. At the time I loved and missed him terribly. Apparently whenever he was in jail, they told me he was on a train trip to Chicago (to this day I have no idea the origins of this story), so whenever I saw a train go by, they say I held out my hands and cried out, "Cago! Cago!"

I think it is important to add here that I deeply loved and still love my dad, his countless faults notwithstanding (he departed this life when I was 26). He had a keen sense of humor and a very kind and generous side to him. And he adored me, as he was able. Of course, there were other grievous aspects to his character and conduct which are not my stories to tell, crimes and abuse, and I'm sure no shortage of victims. Thankfully I never knew about most of them. I simply view him looking back through a lens of compassion, seeing a weak and damaged man, fondly remembering his better nature. I suppose seeing my own failures and wrongs has at some point enabled me to see others as broken children who also grew up into broken adults.

Once, my mom asked my father to step in and help with some matter in which I needed correction. Completely out of character, as he was always joking and virtually never serious, he gave me a sober and intelligent lecture of chastening. I was in shock. Mom was in shock. Then in the silent and serious wake of it, he turned to my mom and asked, "Did I do good, Marga?" I died laughing, while she became furious and chewed him out, as was her custom.

Between her own upbringing in an abusive home during a war, frequent bombing, and her experiences with my dad, my mom was not surprisingly placed in mental institutions on a few occasions after nervous breakdowns, and often heavily medicated at home (I believe Thorazine was the order of the day back then). I heard stories of her sitting for long periods just staring in a prescription drug-induced daze. We were placed in foster care on a few occasions, and my sister tells me I wasn't treated very well. No details given and none sought. Again, let sleeping dogs lie.

Perhaps this would be a good point to pause for a brief interjection.

As I write this, I am in no state of trauma or distress. Quite the contrary. I think back to my mom calling me her "dirty little Mexican" (for the younger readers who are now outraged according to modern customs, it was said affectionately and taken the same way), the smiles of my parents, and even some of the aspects which appear shocking, with a mixture of sadness and love and fondness. While others would find some of these things appalling by standards of Christian decency, they really aren't so uncommon in poor communities. Poverty is seldom merely a matter of financial resource, but frequently part of an entire system of behavior and mindset. My wife and I note at times that I seem to have developed an uncanny ability to not remember bad events, which, coupled with the ability to see negative events in a rather optimistic light, probably account for at least part my favorably skewed view of my own history.

I look back with warmth at things like my first driving lesson. I was probably around fourteen or so when my dad took me to a run-down trailer park, told me to wait in the car, and went inside a trailer. Emerging a little while later bleary-eyed and somewhat slurred in his speech, having just shot up heroin, he said, "You need to drive." Such things to me are something of a darkly comedic parody of what life looks like in the normal world. The warmth of the memory probably stems from the look of bliss on his face and the excitement of the adventure. It was a 1970s huge Ford LTD, and I was all over the road in my steering it as I tried not to hit anyone. I was probably a bit less blissful than he on the short trip home, but elated when we got there and I had driven!

I'm not kidding; that is one of my fondest memories of adolescence. I know my dad was happy, relaxing back into the carelessness of the chemically induced, disconnected state of being, and I was on an adventure usually reserved for those much older.

I should also note, in balance, that I do have many regrets looking back through my life, as I suppose any moral and even mildly introspective person would. Yet I find being intentionally mindful of what is beyond my control, what formative influences caused others to do what they did, my own poor choices as contributing factors as I became able to make them, the reasons for my own choices, and largely an awareness of the limited daily coping resources at my immediate disposal to which I clung—which I am sure kept me from acting on the occasional serious contemplations of suicide—all come together to leave me at a place of acceptance and a degree of gratitude. I have often thought that all things being equal, had I been a man of greater resources, I'd surely have died from excess drug abuse many years ago. And had I been balanced mentally so as to have had some significant success in some vocational pursuit, I'd likely have had the necessary financial resources to fill the much less noticeable God-shaped hole in my soul, and been lost in the more permanent and profound sense. I truly believe the suffering are generally in a better place to know God than the successful. Desperation tends to make us look upwards, while wealth and comfort can tend to make us look sideways toward what we desire in this world.

All things considered, I'm damaged but okay. I'm not here competing for my aluminum medal in the modern victim Olympics.

And besides all this, as I look back, this was merely life. There were hugs and kisses and being adored by my parents, a wonderful relationship with my sister, who was my protector and caretaker much of the time, playing with friends, and ordinary good times as well. I surely have no other life growing up with which to compare it. So, to me this was just childhood. I'm supposing such is likely the case with many who grew up in dysfunctional homes. While others may see the trauma, and rightly so, for us it's not very remarkable, and there are always good times we remember.

Having been a highly gifted student whose name was often the subject of discussion in the teacher's lounge, then dropping out after two and a half intoxicated and useless years of high school may seem to be something I ought to view in retrospect as deeply regrettable.

But it's not so black-and-white for me.

The very torments which I lived on the inside I am convinced drove me to my later need for God. And what good is it to gain the whole world yet lose my own soul? As the mental health struggles continue to this day, so they still keep me keenly aware of my need for God. And for peace.

Okay, back to the story: eventually my mom was befriended by a lovely woman whose family consisted of what were somewhat pillars of the older El Monte decent community. Her help and guidance were the essence of Christian charity. Mrs. Mosely was a godsend to our entire family.

Mom was also approached by the Mormons. For those who don't know, the Mormons had an extremely well organized and effective program to help and train women called Relief Society and cared for their own in very practical and concrete ways. No

Mormon could be left hungry, as they had their own food production and distribution system to care for members of their church.

My mother tried getting her driver's license once, and upon getting her permit, she drove us kids to the store where she promptly turned left in front of someone at an intersection and wrecked the car. Naturally she began yelling at the person for hitting her. That was her last attempt at that. Her nerves were simply not capable of this task. The Mormons would take her grocery shopping and help her with the basic local travel needs associated with simply living life, like doctor's appointments, and helped her establish some sort of moral structure and hope. They were wonderful people overall.

It was in this church which I would be raised for the most part.

As I approached my teenage years my resentment for this world and society increased. A few years ago, I was diagnosed with, among other things, some level of antisocial disorder, which was not surprising. Throughout high school and after I never went to any pep rallies or games or parties. I generally didn't like people. Especially in groups. I didn't like the posturing, vain pursuits, the collective trite values, small and meaningless talk or any of it. Don't get me wrong, I was extremely moral. Always. It's just that my morals were not theirs, and their hypocrisy sickened me.

What was surprising was the unknown (to me) aspect of this disorder—an inability to trust. I simply had never noticed it before. The psychologist asked me to imagine myself as a small child playing at a park. Suddenly a large and threatening dog appeared. Now look immediately to the bench where your caretaker was sitting. What do you see? My bench was empty. This made sense of a lot of my life, and to this day there is almost nobody in this world I really trust. Being poor, there was also nobody to whom I could turn in hard times or financial emergencies. I was always seemingly "on my own." This world has never held much for me, so escaping it through drug abuse was probably a predictable course.

A common Mormon teaching was that we, as spirit children of God pre-existing in heaven, chose our homes and parents. I remember often thinking, "I'm not an idiot! I would have been a dang Rockefeller!"

Once as an adolescent I remember being in a car and noticing the serious and stressful faces on drivers in the other cars. "What are they doing? What is it they're so adamantly pursuing? Money? Why? To buy stuff? What stuff? Are they all crazy? They will be dead soon, and none of that is going with them. This world is utterly shallow and insane."

At the age of twelve, something magical happened. I found a pipe and a little bit of weed hidden in the garage on a high shelf above the washing machine. No doubt it was my dad's. I grabbed a friend and went to a nearby lake and smoked it. After a couple hits, followed by quite a bit of coughing, something amazing happened. For the first time ever, everything got quiet inside. Peace. All the noise and thinking settled down into a present reality where past and future didn't exist. There was only now. And the now was soon filled with incredible laughter. I had found the key to life.

I spent the next two years trying unsuccessfully to find more of this magical substance, and entering summer school before my freshman year of high school, I finally did. A literally unlimited supply. Bag dealers, nickel dealers, dime dealers, and joint dealers. It was everywhere. And an entire community of kids centered around it (though I associated with them, I never had more than one or two close friends). So, I spent the next seventeen years, without exaggeration day and night, excepting a period of a few months which I will mention later, stoned.

I have come to the belief now that drug addicts are people with mental disorders who are simply self-medicating. Only it's not the best medication. What begins as relief or some form of celebration, hedonistic or otherwise, soon descends from euphoria into a coping mechanism which no longer brings elation as it once did, but simply a state in which one can get by. And sadly, even with something so physically non-threatening as marijuana, a cumulative toll begins.

As this sentiment of anger with this world and society increased, and as I nudged slowly toward the age when the Mormons sent us on a two year mission, I left. Two years with no girls and no drugs? No thank you! Besides, there were just too many convoluted beliefs which seemed too far off to have any valuable explanatory power for the state of my life and this world. It all seemed very contrived. I quickly drifted into atheism.

I often said, "If God created this, well, I definitely could have done better." Ironically, claiming He didn't exist, I hated Him at the same time. And the Christian people I saw screaming outside the abortion clinics? Again, no thank you. I despised them.

I spent two and a half years of stumbling stoned from class to class in high school, failing. As an example of what things were like back then at my high school, my daily routine was as follows: slap on some shorts, flip-fop sandals and a Hawaiian shirt, walk to the Mormon Church parking lot a few doors down from the school where the stoners hung out, smoke some weed, stumble into class reeking of marijuana, pass out with my head on the desk, someone would wake me up to go to the next class, then repeat until lunch off campus. Smoke some more weed and repeat again. I remember getting a hall pass from my art teacher so I could go across the street to get a pack of cigarettes. His wife, the teacher's aide, gave me money to grab her a pack while I was there. That was El Monte.

At sixteen I got a summer job at a small shop fixing tent trailers. I immediately excelled and became the shop manager at seventeen, and soon dropped out of high school (for all practical purposes, my formal education ended after the eighth grade). This was the first time I saw the value of the work ethic my mother had instilled in me. Probably the first time I appreciated her at all. I had come to really resent her and her hard-nosed German upbringing during my teenage years. Things like having to redo all the dishes when a speck was found on one had taken a toll of deep animosity. She was absolutely uncompromising and unyielding. To this day, however, I swear the work ethic my mother instilled in me was the only thing that kept me from going over the edge with drug abuse. I'd have done better coming home telling her I was just arrested for some heinous crime than being fired from a job. I never missed work, no matter how tore up I was from one substance or another. And I always did it well.

At twenty I met a girl, my cocktail waitress, as I hadn't been asked for ID at a bar since I was about 19, and not too long after, we moved in together.

Chapter 2

"You have not abandoned us to the end. . ."

However you sort through the next part of the story, however you choose to characterize it through your theological lens, is up to you. I will only tell it as I experienced it. I was about twenty-two at the time.

My then girlfriend and I lived in a fourplex apartment in El Monte (yeah, still in that charming little town) with Christian neighbors directly above us. We had never met the husband, since he was a truck driver who had been on the road since we moved in, as explained by his wife with whom occasional weed sales exchanges occurred. Once I found out she was a Christian, I sometimes chided her about believing in all that nonsense. She would always respond, "Wait until Theo (her husband) comes back. Talk to him."

After going on a vacation to Utah with my girlfriend, the most miserable experience imaginable as we fought almost the whole time, I decided it was time to go.

Not wanting another major fight, I set a plan to pack it up while she was working her cocktail shirt Friday night and move in with my or sister.[1]

---

[1] I'm guessing it was from my experience in foster care that I developed this sense of urgency to flee from situations I considered unsafe, that assessment being always on the side distrust, and so I became a "runner" of sorts. Before Anastasia I had never been with any woman (and believe

That Friday at work something happened which changed the direction of my life and worldview.

While working at the shop, someone in a truck pulled up to our propane station to have his tanks filled for work. A beautiful yellow dog (her coat and build appeared to be those of a German Shepherd/Yellow Labrador mix) jumped out of his truck and refused to go back in. He explained that he had to go back to work, and that the dog had jumped in the cab back at his job and he had never seen her before. So off he went.

As she went into the shop area, everyone stopped to pet her, as did I, but she attached herself to me. Everywhere I went that day she followed. It looked like I now had a dog. But wait. I can't take her to my mom or sister's house. Now what of my escape plan? I supposed I'd have to wait a bit longer to devise a new strategy.

The next morning (when I should have been gone) Theo the truck driver who lived upstairs, arrived home from the road. I went up to meet him, bringing some really good weed, as is the communal practice of stoners. We sat and smoked a few bowls, then I asked, "So you are a Christian? What do you believe?" He responded, "I believe the Bible is true." And with that I asked what he thought it said. He began a narrative of creation and human history, I stopping him frequently to test if what he was relaying was in fact what the book said. "Show me that," I would say. He in turn flipping to a page and reading the text which matched his telling of the story. Having become convinced he

---

me, I was with a lot of them) more than a few months before being overcome with a sense of suffocation, as if I was trapped. Such was my normal state throughout the nine years of my first marriage.

was offering a fair representation of the narrative, I sat back and listened.

I suppose I need to mention here that ten minutes after smoking some really good weed with him, I was sober as a judge. And I knew it. This was shocking, but I kept it to myself.

At one point I challenged him with my most deeply seated resentment regarding God: the issue of pain and suffering. The answer he offered was sufficient to make sense of things from that framework, absolve God, and remove the barrier to my hearing the story he was offering (I truly believe that while Apologetics is not the way into the Kingdom, it serves to remove the roadblocks to that path). I even asked him about smoking weed as a Christian, to which he flipped to Genesis 1 and had me read: "I give you every plant that has seeds for food," then he asked, "What happens if you eat this?" Well, that was good enough for me. Pot brownies get you high too. And so, he spoke and I listened and asked questions for several hours. And I went home. (I believe I had been up to this point under a certain grace, not having known better, and doing my best with what I understood. Later I came to discover why intoxicants were disharmonious with the life of a Christian. And much later, up learning and becoming Orthodox, I learned of the larger problem with literalist interpretations of scripture).

The next evening, the same. We sat and smoked some weed, he began telling me more; again, in ten minutes I was *sober*, and again, I had my newfound dog with me on a leash. Before I left, he asked me, "Would you like to receive Jesus as your personal Lord and Savior?" My mind raced around my life. It was pretty good overall. Certainly, there were no catastrophes to induce my abandoning it. My best friend, who was a Vietnam vet whom I loved like a brother, a stoner buddy, also an atheist, came to mind.

I knew this would sever our friendship, and I was in no way wanting that. So, I politely declined.

The next evening, repeat. Same thing. Same weed. Same sobriety. Same topic of discussion. At the end of the evening this time, however, he said, "I have never said this to anyone before but what guarantee do you have that when you leave my apartment tonight you will not fall down the stairs and break your neck?"

"None," I replied, being a very logically oriented person.

"Where would you go?" he asked. I sat and thought about my life and my best friend. There would be loss, but I have no guarantee of tomorrow, and eternity is forever. I said to myself, "Nobody is worth going to hell over."

I replied, "I am ready."

He proceeded to lead me in a prayer, and something happened. Something I cannot begin to adequately explain. Something which I could only describe as permeating my being from the marrow of my bones to the hairs on my body. I didn't say anything to anyone about it though.

No, not emotion. It wasn't that. I had come to know the basic spectrum of emotions, as I suppose we all do while fairly young, from the depths of despair to the greatest of joys, and this was not that. Any of it. It was beyond. Other. And it was accompanied by a knowing. A clarity.

Leaving his apartment with my dog, she spotted a cat. I kept her leash wrapped around my wrist, and as she launched into her pursuit, I flew from about the midpoint of the staircase to the concrete below, landing squarely on my feet, immediately remembering what he had just said. It seemed pretty clear this was a confirmation.

Chapter 3

"You have manifested Yourself to us, who were sitting in darkness and the shadow of death."

Over the next couple of days this thing that happened to me remained. That sense of almost not being physically present in my life, as if just floating along as an observer of sorts. And everything, I mean everything, acted as if it was all lined up for me, being orchestrated. Red lights all turned green. Everything was effortless. I was installing a bracket on a truck axle and dropped a bolt. It fell in the hole about a foot below, where it belonged. Let me tell you, I've been wrenching for over forty years, and that has never before or since happened. And in all this, something was speaking throughout telling me these were not coincidences. They were all confirmations. (I later came to believe the reason such extraordinary signs were given to me were because of my extreme tendency to abandon things and unusually low propensity for faith. He met me where I was, as I was seeking in all sincerity, and gave me what He knew I needed to be able to remain in my belief in Christ for the rest of my life. I invite the reader to make sense of it all however seems best to you).

We met at Theo's place every night, spending hours in Bible studies. Just he, his wife, and I. For months this went on, seven nights a week. Early in this period he baptized me in his bathtub. Seems about right for El Monte.

At some point a few months in, I sensed what seemed to be a figurative tap on the shoulder. It was about the weed. "That's in the way. Get rid of it." Not so much as, "It's bad," more like, "That's a hindrance." So I did. And there was no struggle involved.

To those reading who have never been addicts, there's just no way to explain the miraculous nature of something like this. See, we drug addicts all have our "drug of choice," that one substance which matches our chemistry in such a way as creates something almost euphoric at the introduction, and makes daily life tolerable as we settle into it over time. Self-medication. Remove it, and life becomes sheer torment. Simple, daily, ordinary life becomes almost unbearable. For me, ordinary daily life was worse than unusually stressful events. I'd rather have been in the waves of a tempest than in the stillness of the doldrums. To have my medication removed after years of literal around-the-clock use and have no negative effects is something I will always consider beyond natural explanation.

After some months of nightly bible studies, seven nights a week, a rift was sewn. Since I have no intent or desire to tell anyone else's story here, much less to bash anyone, I'll just say we became estranged.

Not too long afterwards my first wife (by that time we had gotten married) and I moved to a house. Though I had fallen away from bible study and prayer, my belief in who He was never changed. On the other hand, my lifestyle certainly did. But this did fit with the theology I had been taught up to this point: believing is what saves us, not doing. There was no real sense of urgency regarding works as long as I believed. I can say in all sincerity that at any point since that prayer at Theo's apartment, had anyone put a gun to my head and demanded I deny that Jesus is the Christ, I'd have said, "You'll have to shoot, because I can't do that."

Trying to get back up and walk in my faith again seemed impossible, though I tried a number of times before giving up. Slowly I drifted back into drug use. (I suppose this is a good time to mention that while marijuana was my staple daily, I used virtually any drug I could get my hands on at various times in my life. I used everything from hallucinogens to barbiturates to amphetamines, some for prolonged periods, with the exception of heroin and PCP. I had seen what heroin did to my dad, and witnessed the old "dusters," people who used PCP, or Angel Dust, becoming almost senile after not many years of use. Needles were even used on a few occasions).

I recall one evening, sometime after moving into this home, when we had a young Latino gang member living next door. I hadn't done cocaine in a number of years and he and his friends were dealing it. During my heavy cocaine period the high had deteriorated from being a semi-euphoric state to an absolutely anxiety-ridden paranoid one, culminating in my spending two weeks with some friends at the Kern River, during which time I took large amounts of barbiturates to withdraw from the coke. But that was years ago. Maybe now I could go recapture that first high?

After taking a sizable amount, my wife being at work, the anxiety came back as hard as ever. It was like the last time, not the first. I went to lay down in the bedroom to calm back down, and as the anxiety grew there also grew a deep aching, paralyzing pain in my left arm which spread through the left side of my body and continued moving rightward. I had a deep and clear sense that I was having a heart attack, and once this pain spread over to the other side, I'd be dead. I can't say how I knew, but I just did.

I called upon Christ repeatedly, knowing this was my only hope, and it began to subside, retreating along the same path till it left entirely. That was the last time I used cocaine. Such was one experience of this isolated, groping, yet still believing period.

This all culminated in a very bad marriage. And again, this is not about anyone else's story, only mine. I'll gladly admit I had been a lousy and emotionally inaccessible husband.

At the age of 31, with a young child and an unhappy wife, I became aware that my marriage had been dying unnoticed in front of me. It was as if I was just waking up from a night's sleep to find the world had completely changed, and there was nothing I could do to get it back. Though I desperately tried, the hopelessness of the situation arose suddenly before me, naturally for a time blaming the spouse. But that was of no benefit regarding the relief I needed. I began earnestly seeking God again. Only this time it was different.

As I sat on the floor of my bedroom staring at the shotgun next to the bed, planning how to take it out the window and go down the street and kill myself, so as not to traumatize my child and make a mess, I wept bitterly asking God, *"Help me!"*

Though not audible, the conversation we had was clear and unmistakable.

"You want my help?"

"Yes."

"Really?"

"YES!"

"Okay. Here it is. You've been rude."

"I've been rude. Yes."

"You've been hurtful."

"I've been hurtful. Yes."

And so, on and on it went. I can't remember the whole list, but it was extensive.

At the end I felt empty. Hollow. Barren. Aching. But the extreme, intolerable anguish had subsided. I smoked some weed in an attempt to obtain some inward sense of normalcy. It did nothing to assuage the deep relentless pain. Looked like it was time to lay it down again. I mean, what was the point if it wasn't helping?

The next day, Monday, I had this overwhelming desire to tell someone what I had done. Keep in mind I was an Evangelical Christian, so I had no context or idea why. I simply had a compelling urge to tell someone of my sins.

First, I went to a large church someone had recommended years earlier (I had not as yet been to a church as a Christian) but they were closed. Nobody was there. Then I went to what I had called the church of the parking lot beggars, since my only experience with them was their asking for donations in parking lots for their missionary work, and there I found someone. A young, sincere, and committed Hispanic man.

We sat and talked and I told him everything. He admonished me that suicide was an unforgivable sin, which was useless advice since I was already past that, and overall, he had nothing of any value to impart, excepting of course a pair of ears and a sincere heart, which was apparently exactly what I needed. There was a huge sense of relief as I left. I knew I was supposed to do this, though not understanding why, and I began to feel less hollow. So, I returned home.

Through many discussions with God at that time, my perception of His position was always consistent. Never was I allowed to point to anyone's sins but my own. He would say things like, "You didn't take a vow simply not to beat her up or cheat. You promised to love and cherish, and you did not. So, you have no case to make in your own defense. You can't accuse her of breaking a covenant which you never upheld." I was prompted to serve her at home and be silent, and did so as much as I was able, until circumstances became unbearable (for reasons which I won't share) to the point where I left the home. To this day I thank God for that season, as it left me with some sense of having truly done my best, albeit too little too late. Not absolution, but mitigation, which was enough. I mean, it had to be. It was all I had.

Now living with my nephew, I looked back at times I tried to walk with God and failed. It became apparent what I lacked: a support community of believers. So, I decided it was time to try church.

Chapter 4

"Let us attend."

The first time I walked into an Evangelical church, it was a fairly large one, the interior being in the midst of development, as one area within the large former aerospace structure was being transformed into a permanent sanctuary.[2] We met in what would soon be the gymnasium after the other area, which was under construction, was completed. I had a strong sense that this was what I needed, and as time went on, I became acutely aware that I couldn't live this life without such a support system and frequent attendance.

At first simply attending, I soon was called upon by my sister, who was also an attendee, to help with a ministry for special needs kids. This was her weekday occupation, and in the evangelical world they appeared to be one of the only desperately needed locations for worshipers to drop their high maintenance children for a time of worship and teaching. I usually got the same young boy, around six or so years old, who was extreme ADHD. Being the only male, and in fairly good shape at the time, I seemed well suited to the high-speed pursuits through the halls of the vast building as he got his pent-up energy released. Before long, and I can't remember what prompted it, I began ushering.

Meeting in this rectangular room, which was wider than it was deep, with as I recall a seating capacity of around a thousand,

---

[2] Note to Orthodox readers: what is here referred to as a sanctuary is essentially what you would call the nave. Ironically, in the churches with altar calls there is no altar, only a stage.

we filled to overflow at the main Sunday service. The rows being very long, and people tending to leave a seat or two open between themselves and those already seated when they arrived, there tended to be quite a few individual open seats in each row. The ushers would try to get people to scoot down and fill the empties, often to no avail. Except in my section.

See, I tended to be a rather thuggish looking figure, wearing sleeveless button-down shirts and jeans, tattooed, yet also had a very pleasant and warm demeanor as I served. Nobody likes to say no to a pleasant thug who is asking nicely. I developed my own technique: instead of asking people to scoot, I would ask (mostly through hand motions) if there was an empty next to them (I would hold up a finger or two indicating the number of empty seats as it seemed from my vantage point, and point with a questioning expression on my face), and when they said, "Yes," I would then ask them to scoot in and fill it. Once they acknowledge the empty seat, it's hard to say no or pretend not to notice the person asking.

Noting my effectiveness, all the ushers had me coming over to their sections to assist them in filling gaps. I became known as The Squisher. I consider this the phase when I went from being a believer to being a servant and a church member. I'll never forget the words of Pastor Chuck, who oversaw the ushers, father of the head pastor. His credentials basically were his business, a Union 76 gas station which he owned and operated for many years (that was the epitome of customer service in the olden days), God rest his soul. He told me, "You start becoming a true servant when you don't mind being treated like one." A hard pill to swallow, but a necessary one. Before long I was also asked to run the Wednesday night service ushers, as I was always in attendance anyway.

Moving into the now completed new sanctuary, seating 2489 (I still remember that capacity), the extra seating did not last long. As the church grew rapidly, we began televising (a recorded TV program centered around the sermon), and with that came new challenges, fully explaining which would be beyond the scope of this writing. I will simply say that camera shots panning filled sections, nobody moving or walking through a camera shot, small windows of opportunity to identify and fill individual and double open seats, and crying babies were all needing to be addressed. So, I had an idea.

I created and implemented a team of seaters, all wearing earpieces, with people at the doors and beginnings of aisles (two of each), with a three staged flow direction and filling strategy, and I up in the riser seat aisle viewing the bigger picture and directing. All this was done based on voluntary cooperation from the congregation (60-70% compliance was expected). Anyone who ignored us and went wherever they chose were free to do so. This team was separate from the regular ushers (part of the reason for this was the window of time when they were collecting offerings was the last opportunity we had to squish and fill, and they were busy). This plan worked remarkably well. We had single digit empties (often 3-5) in sections of 250 or more seats.

In addition to this, I was still running the Wednesday night service, and was asked to run the seating at all special events: Hillsong concerts, celebrity pastors (which often attracted celebrity guests whom I won't name, but you'd know. Some famous and some infamous. One name I will mention since this was his regular church home is Terry Crews. Yes, he's all you've heard in his gentility, goodness and humility. And more than you have heard. His wife had a heart of gold as well), and celebrity speakers. At first this was all very exciting, but one thing kept getting to me, regarding the church's handling of these events: reserved seats for big donors and celebrities.

Regarding the crowds, we ushers were often appalled by common occurrences like someone waiting hours for us to open, then running through the church to get a prime seat (somehow nearer to God? I have no idea), placing his Bible on his seat, going to the bathroom, and returning to find someone in the seat with the Bible they had left now sitting on the floor, saying they didn't know how it got there. But none of this was the fault of leadership; I suppose it's all just an unavoidable part of religious celebrity culture.

When there was a special event, one big name faith healer in particular, as many as a couple hundred seats were reserved for the "important people," as lines formed at times down the block. And being important, they didn't have time for the worship part. (In Protestant Evangelical services, the first 30 or so minutes is dedicated to singing a mixture of upbeat and reflective songs. The time is called Praise and Worship, or simply Worship.) These "important people" only came for the big show, arriving about 45 minutes or more late, as we kept holding their seats.

Funny side story: on one such occasion of the big faith healer, as I would often be a "catcher" (that guy who catches people when they fall backwards under the Holy Ghost), I arrived feeling great. One woman behind whom I stood, ready to catch her (my record was a guy who weighed 280 lbs.!), convulsed and I caught her boney elbow in my eye. I thought, "Well isn't that special. They come sick and leave healed and I come healthy and leave with a shiner!"

I began discussing this issue with a lovely lady who handled the reserved seating list, who likewise wasn't too fond of the whole thing. But she would shrug and say, "Not our decision."

This culminated in one such event which prompted me to write a letter to the head pastor in which I cited James 2:3.[3] I was literally seating people on the floor while holding seats for the "important" (read: wealthy and/or famous) people for nearly an hour. He did call me to meet with him, was sympathetic, and made a few minor adjustments, telling me I was the best usher this church had ever had. Yet the Sunday big donor seating issue remained unchanged.

Finally, it bothered me enough that I stepped down.

Toward the end of this period of my life, while still attending this megachurch, I met Michelle (who became my wife, Anastasia). She was a Wednesday night regular. When the head pastor's brother split off to begin his own smaller and more organic feeling church, we soon followed. And remained there for a time. It felt much better than what we had left. Pastor Bob, who is now reposed, was a wonderful, accessible, and caring man. Then one of his pastors, with whom I had become very close, split off and began an even smaller and more organic church, so off we went again. Before meeting Coptic priests, Pastor Joel was the best shepherd I had ever met. He would even drop by my work unannounced just to see how I was doing.

During this season, now being in my early forties, Anastasia and I watched a Christian video teaching series in which the host

---

[3] In a megachurch you do not have access to the top man. You certainly do not have the cell phone numbers of the top people like you do an Orthodox priest. He also has escorts to keep the congregation from having direct access to him.

spoke of colonial America and their intellect levels. He showed the New England Primer, from which small children learned to read, and other examples of writings directed at farmers. Anastasia remarked, "When we speak of Homer, we mean Simpson. What happened?" It occurred to us that something had definitely gone wrong, and we began to question what had changed. We asked ourselves what was different about their lives, and modern media/entertainment quickly came to mind. So, we decided on an experiment: one week with no media. No TV, no computer, nothing. We had no plan beyond that. No idea what we would do. No goal.

The first evening I picked up a book on an apologetics subject (apologetics here means defense of the Christian faith). It had been many years since I'd read a book, and decades before that book to the one before. Within a couple minutes I was bored, figuring I wouldn't finish it anyway, and set it back down. Within a couple more minutes I picked it back up, realizing I had nothing else to do. It drew me in and I finished it, piquing my interest more deeply regarding Christian apologetics.

At the time I had a Myspace account (yeah, that long ago), and they had debate/discussion forums. Religion and Philosophy caught my attention. I began engaging. At first, it was terrifying. Virtually every atheist/agnostic I encountered was a former evangelical Christian. And to this day, some of the most knowledgeable and well-studied challengers to my faith I've ever known, often sharper than most celebrity atheists you see today. Each new comment or subject I encountered shook my faith deeply. Profoundly. Knowing which Christian apologists tended to be the best in a given area, I'd order a book, often only needing a chapter or so to discover the most compelling answer to the challenge. I felt a bit more secure in my faith after each exchange than I had before. And I do mean a bit. And so it went, subject after subject, post after post (being forum settings, rather than chats, there was time to go research). I remember the fear which gripped me each time I turned on my computer, not knowing what I would find. Trying to be intellectually honest, and at the same time opening yourself up to critical challenges, is no endeavor for the faint of heart. While each answer instilled some level of confidence, that increase is minor in relation to the fear arising with each new unfamiliar claim for quite some time. But over the two years of four to eight hours a day, seven days a week, of this endeavor, my confidence did grow, to the point near the end that I had a certain inward settling that whatever I encountered would have a good answer. I only needed to go find it. My little library of apologetics grew, along with a bit of knowledge.

Then came an unexpected day.

I went to the forum, began scrolling new posts, and something surprising hit me: there was nothing new to me. Sure, maybe some mild variant on some issue I'd previously discussed, but nothing really new. I leaned back in my chair and said to myself, "I think I'm done." I turned off my computer.

During this period of study, which I later looked back on as my third phase (after believer, then servant), that of a learner, Anastasia and I began helping out in the high school/college group ministry. Little did we know the paths to which this seemingly simple decision would soon lead. Having become fairly well known as very knowledgeable in our faith (at times the pastor would have me review his sermon notes to check for theological errors), after one youth meeting a college kid asked, "If God knows everything that's going to happen, why do we pray?"

I responded, "There is a pretty good answer to that question, but not a five minute one."

I went on to explain how every Friday night Anastasia and I would go to the nearby Starbucks, order a drink and sit outside. I'd have a cigar, and we would talk about God. I asked if she'd like to join us and we could discuss it then. She agreed. We also invited anyone else interested in attending to join us as well. About a half dozen showed up. And so was born Theology Night each Friday from 7-10 pm.[4]

Theology Night quickly grew to between a dozen and a few dozen weekly, at times having a guest join us for a given topic. Subjects ranged from theology to apologetics. I even invited a sharp Calvinist to come argue against my more Arminian views for the group to hear both sides and encounter a quality discussion of disagreement. Kids under 18 years old (we had a few as young as junior high) had to get special permission from their parents since I and a couple others smoked cigars at our sessions.

One of those evenings a young lady asked a question which seemed simple enough, but had an unexpectedly profound impact which would set me on the path I walk today.

"How did we get our Bible?"

---

[4] I understand the limited attention span issues people face in giving lessons, but using the discussion format and a flexibility to go off in any direction the group finds interesting, rather than rigidly sticking to a lesson plan or topic, had us going for three hours each week, often followed by returning to our place for a few more hours. Similarly, today when I speak to groups with an open-ended time frame, they aren't usually finished for three to four hours. Once in Cairo, we held an open-ended time lecture/discussion for six hours.

Remembering an unread book on the subject sitting on my shelf by F.F. Bruce called *The Canon of Scripture*, I went over and grabbed it for her.[5]

"Why don't you read this and give us all this lesson?"

She took it, then returned it after a few weeks.

"Yeah, no. I can't."

And so, it fell back on me.

After a few months and three passes through the book I was ready. The lesson took eighteen hours (six three-hour sessions) and I had produced a thirty-two-page handout. One profound realization was that unlike my modern paradigm, in which we were looking to the Bible to find out what was true, the early Church looked at the truth they were given (as codified in the creeds, liturgies, oral tradition, etc.) to determine what was Bible, having no established canon of scripture for a few centuries. They also looked back into the Old Testament not so much to find unknown truth, but more viewed it through the established lens of the truth of Christ they had received, to discover and affirm Him there.

I was not only surprised by what I found, but more importantly I had come into my first real meaningful contact with the early church. The formation of the Bible as a canon of scripture is primarily set in the first four centuries. And it wasn't so simple and clean as one might imagine. Yet in this process of discovery, I met some figures who truly impacted me, like Saint Athanasius of Alexandria. Yet none more profoundly life changing than Saint Irenaeus of Lyons. In the context of the

---

[5] F. F. Bruce, *The Canon of Scripture* (Downers Grove: IVP Academic, 1988).

formation of the canon, his primary point was, "All the churches hold the same writings. The Gnostic ones are not ours."

Chapter 5

"Look towards the East."

Saint Irenaeus was a disciple of Saint Polycarp, Bishop of Smyrna in modern-day Turkey and himself a disciple of the Apostle John. He was also very familiar with the Church of Rome. This meant he had a broad exposure to the churches over a substantially large region. Keep in mind that travel and communication was not as it is today, so each church operated more independently.

Saint Irenaeus authored his works around 180 AD battling against Gnostics groups. These rather Platonist groups with a dualist theology (a sharp divide between the perfect spiritual and the fallen physical) claimed to have the "secret" and elite teachings passed down from the Apostles, which were kept from the ordinary masses who lacked the special sophistication to handle them. They produced a number of manuscripts which they attributed to New Testament figures (like Thomas, Peter, etc.) for legitimacy. For the most part, what we knew of these sects came from Saint Irenaeus' writings against them prior to the twentieth century discovery of the Nag Hammadi library in Egypt, which held a historical treasure trove of their texts.

His argument was so simple and so compelling.

At this early stage of the Church, the Apostles had traveled the known world and preached the gospel. They spent years and years with these individual communities and traveled between them. They personally taught them the Christian beliefs and practices, and on occasion sent letters back to the churches dealing with various issues which arose, encouraging and instructing them, relying on their prior shared experiences and teachings as the context for these communications. These communities copied the letters and shared them with each other. They also selected bishops from among the congregations to oversee them, stringent qualifications needing to be met, some of which can be found in the New Testament writings themselves. These bishops were personally trained and established by the Apostles, with the consent of the people, and were to be kept as offices in a perpetual succession of authority. At times this succession was fairly rapid, as becoming a bishop often was a death sentence due to persecution. Not really something to which the average person would be expected to aspire for purposes of prestige.

Saint Irenaeus argued simply (paraphrased): "Go to any community of the Christians, which had been set up by the Apostles, whose bishops they had chosen, and ask what they believe. Ask to see their writings. You will find the same beliefs and writings in them all. And you will also find that none had ever so much as heard of these Gnostic beliefs and writings. Surely if the Apostles were to leave an important deposit of crucial information essential to salvation, they would have entrusted these to the communities they established and the bishops they chose." This hit me like a ton of bricks.

Being a fairly knowledgeable American Evangelical, I was well aware of the countless schisms of the West. The endless verse versus verse arguments between groups demonstrating how their interpretations of scripture were the correct ones, offering up plain readings of proof verses while explaining away the proof verses of the competitors through contextual gymnastics. Each group had no shortage of good, sincere, and well-studied "scholars" to defend the primacy of their interpretation. Yet the end result was a virtual theological Babel—everyone speaking in a different language. Surely if God had intended this book to stand above the churches as a sole guide, something went horribly wrong.

Anastasia and I had already experienced no small discomfort at the entertainment/market researched/customer service/business competitor model of American evangelical churches. I had just for the first time read the letter of Saint Ignatius (also a disciple of Saint John the Apostle) the Bishop of Antioch to the Church of Rome, being profoundly moved by the entirely different "flavor" and ethos[6] than that to which I had become accustomed as an American Evangelical. I found myself enthralled at the idea of reading the thoughts of a disciple of an Apostle. While the deep roots to the early Church and the discovery of the mindset of this remarkable early Church figure captivated me, as I gained the clarity of the best way to proceed with a logical inquiry using a concrete and intelligent methodology, some decided efforts were required to put such personal, subjective impacts aside for a time.

I was seeking truth, not personal satisfaction.

And here I now stood. The clear and decisive true north to my compass to be used in pursuing the Christian faith seemed evident in that one simple question: what did the communities

---

[6] I use this term over and over in this book. I understand it as the undefined summary of the faith, in terms of the spirit of the teachings and practice. The flavor, the smell, the unspoken underlying foundation to all things conveyed. When we hear something which seems odd, but also true, and cannot quite put our finger on what is off about it, that is the different ethos. And even if we do not know why it does not fit, though someone perhaps more theologically astute or bilingual may, we just instinctively can tell it is not "ours." It is the "vibe."

and bishops of the early Church believe and what were their practices?

You see, if any universal voice could be found, to which Saint Irenaeus seemed to point, there were only two possible explanations as far as I could tell.

> 1. This was what the Apostles taught.
> 2. All the communities they had trained and all the bishops they selected (or their immediate successors) decided to replace the original teachings with the exact same alternate ones, rather independently and by unanimous consent. All with no objections.

Having not met Eastern Christians yet, I did encounter one story in my study of the formation of the canon which struck me as humorous, one which only had a clear context and implications regarding the fierce defense of and fidelity to tradition, after I got to know the Copts.

It seems in Saint Jerome's translation of scripture, in which he used the Masoretic Hebrew text rather than the standard Greek Septuagint, he translated the plant under which Jonah sat as an ivy rather than a gourd.[7] Saint Augustine wrote him to complain that when this translation was read at church, there broke out a riot in the city.[8] Today I can see if someone changed something in the liturgy, among the Egyptian-raised Copts that such an outbreak might occur, probably led by the old grandmothers throwing shoes and the uncles tearing their *tonias* (a white robe worn by those serving at the liturgy). If there is any honest criticism to be offered of such types, it would be clinging to

---

[7] F.F. Bruce, *The Canon of Scripture,* (Downers Grove: InterVarsity Press, 1988), 94.
[8] Ibid.

customs as if they were dogma, and not an inflated sense of liberty to innovate or abrogate.

The idea of basic beliefs easily and universally being overthrown in communities whose fidelity could be seen in their willingness (at times to the point of being perhaps too eager) to suffer tortures and death is simply beyond ridiculous, as is the notion of the Apostles having neglected clarity of teaching in such basic tenets of the faith. Likewise, the lack of any record of these controversies, amid the mountains of writings regarding every other controversy, is absurd.[9]

Attempting here to be as intellectually honest as I could, I decided to set up a methodology and data prior to embarking on the quest to answer the question, "What was the Christianity taught by the Apostles to the churches?" Setting up a standard of testing prior to viewing the data, then trying to maintain adherence to it, seemed to me the best safeguard against merely collecting evidence to affirm what I may want, intentionally or not, to be true. I was prepared to leave Protestantism if needed,

---

[9] It is a rule of mine (which I too often break) that it is futile to have a meaningful discussion with someone who claims to be unbiased. If one is this deeply un-self-aware, as we all have biases, it is nearly impossible to make such a person aware of something he finds undesirable which is outside of himself. Therefore, entering into this endeavor with a mindfulness of my own bias was essential, as much as I was able. I believe this to be a fundamental marker of the difference between seeking truth and seeking affirmation of that which one finds comforting and/or appealing, along with seeking contrary and opposed sources and views to consider. A good general rule is this: come to terms of acceptance with possible outcomes of an inquiry before beginning. Otherwise, we are not really asking honestly. I have freely admitted to atheist friends that I cannot give their arguments a fair and honest hearing. The implications of there being no God, the utter meaningless futility of everything in such a case, is more than I could bear and still live a life that pushes through hardships. I know I am not intellectually open to their claims, and I openly acknowledge it.

though I did not expect to, but at the time I was unaware of an impending interim period which I will discuss later.

The methodology was this: seek the universal voice where it could be found. This meant the earlier the better, the longer it was sustained the better. If this was indeed the church established by Christ, and if the Holy Spirit was given to them as a whole, then the universal voice, where it could be found, would be that of the Spirit. As the universality decreased on a given topic, so would the centrality and certainty of the belief.

Allowance would be made for later emerging controversies and expanded understandings, looking for universality and endurance after the dust settled in such cases. This methodology would stand in contrast to the Roman Papist view, in which one man was the ultimate spokesman for the Spirit, and the Protestant view in which the canon of scripture, whose contents and authorship they do not seem to notice hinge on the trustworthiness of the earlier Christians, not even seeming to be aware of the biases imposed on the texts via personal interpretations, is that voice.[10]

The data was this: early Christian writings.

At the same time as I began this research endeavor, I entered an Orthodox Church to learn about it and do a parallel inquiry of beliefs and practices, in person, of this ancient "branch" (as I

---

[10] I think the fierce defense and at times, in my opinion, acrobatics involved in proving the inerrancy of the Papacy by the one and the scriptures by the other are a result of these houses of cards. No errors can be acknowledged without infallibility being lost. In juxtaposition we Orthodox, should we encounter an error in scripture or by a Church Father, could simply say, "Okay, no big deal. We look to the whole for our guidance. Any small or singular aberrations do not change that. Further, the rest of the writings and thoughts by the one who committed errors could be retained, if verified by the broader voice of the whole."

understood it to be at the time) of Christianity. While the encounter and experiences were paralleled chronologically, it seems best to separate the experiential side of this journey from the truth-pursuit intellectual endeavor, to some extent. Therefore, I'll return to this point of the story, chronologically, and restart the path through a parallel, personal experience narrative later on.

Having sought out an Orthodox Church, I met a young priest, Abouna (Father) Daniel, whom I hoped could assist me in this pursuit of discovering, testing, and parsing truth claims which I surely would encounter. Unfortunately, he was not of much help with a sizable amount of the work ahead, for understandable reasons. While perfectly willing to help in any way possible, what stood before him was not a blank sheet of paper. In fact, it was rather well written, only in a different (Protestant) language, and while many terms were the same, the meanings and contexts were most disparate. He spoke fluent *Orthodox*, I spoke fluent *Protestant*, and neither of us was theologically bilingual. I had an entire coherent system of beliefs going in. Which of the beliefs were harmonious? Which were not? And why not? Why are they wrong? Why are yours right? And so on.

Clearly it is easier to fill a blank page with writing than to erase large portions, keeping some, and rewriting the rest.

All I could get from him was: "This is what we believe." He had no training or understanding in Protestantism, but certainly embodied the Orthodox ethos, beliefs, and approach to things. In this regard, to this day I could think of no better guide regarding the acquisition of the Orthodox mindset. His Orthodoxy was so deeply rooted in and reflective of the deep ancient ethos that, on my trip some years later to Saint Macarius Monastery in Egypt, being asked to sit in a room with eighteen monks to tell my story and answer questions, to my answers one remarked afterwards,

"You are *very* Orthodox." To which I replied, "If anything in me is Orthodox, it's because of my Abouna who taught me."

You see, it's not merely about the answers to questions from an Orthodox perspective. It's largely about which questions are relevant, how to ask, and the underlying premises and mindset in the asking. As Abouna Daniel once told me, "We don't study the Fathers to gain the words of the Fathers, but the mind of the Fathers." There comes a way of thinking and speaking which is just recognized and known by the Orthodox, and when someone speaks from the point of a different paradigm, it is just recognized as *other*. One need not even be able to explain why. It just fails the smell test, as it were. It is indeed, in a very real sense, a different language.

Another key influence whom I met early and proved enduring was a man called upon by Abouna Daniel to help answer my questions, Emmanuel Gergis. Being himself on a journey of theological knowledge inside the Orthodox Church, we immediately clicked. Like Abouna Daniel, he was able to help me with obtaining Orthodox beliefs, yet unable to speak Protestant, or even Western (in terms of thought and approach) very fluently. The thing which was different was his eagerness to engage in hot debates over the questions, and a desire to learn these alternate means of expression and inquiry. Hours at a time we would haggle and argue, arms and hands waving, sharing a common zeal for truth itself (consulting with him during the writing of this book, he reminded me of some F-bombs I dropped in these heated discussions and informed me that at one point he almost feared for his life). Such a process at the end left us both fairly theologically bilingual, not only in terms and beliefs, but also in an ability to view things from both a mystical and an intellectually parsing point of view.

Manny (Emmanuel) would later become my godfather and a PhD theologian.

For the rest of the sorting and answering process I seemed to be on my own. Thank God for the internet!

Finding other communities which actually had "study-in" converts (mostly former Protestants), and not just a few odd Americans who had fallen in love with a woman of foreign descent (the only Americans I had met at the time in the Coptic Church), I was able get in touch with some people (frequently, though not exclusively, from the Antiochian Orthodox Church) and articles which were written by theologically bilingual astute Orthodox. There remain to this day, again understandably so, a scarce few in the Coptic world.

Here are my first discoveries, applying the established methodology.

Baptism

Since this seems the entry point for the historic church into the faith, what was it? Was it simply an outward profession of the reality which had occurred already when one had responded to an altar call (a relatively recent western phenomenon in which one joins in a recited prayer, inviting Jesus into your heart, following which one is pronounced forgiven and now "saved?" Yet Saint Peter in the Book of Acts, when asked, "What must we do to be saved?" did not say, "Repeat this prayer after me…" but rather, "Repent and be baptized"). Was it merely an outward symbol of a regeneration which had already occurred by faith and confession of Jesus as Lord? Or was it the point of regeneration, the very ontological entry into the living Body of Christ (John 3:5), the Church, as circumcision was the entry into the community of God in the Old Testament (Colossians 2:11-12)? My research led me to the latter being the case.

Even in the fairly brief period of controversy over infant baptism, when many would wait on baptism until the person had sown their wild oats, or in the case of some like Constantine, waited till the death bed, both sides argued based on the acknowledgement of its salvific efficacy, prior to the settled and enduring unbroken continuity of affirming the practice. You see, there was a basic understanding that one who was enlightened and entered into Christ, should he fall away, could become irretrievable (Hebrews 6:4-6). What that point of permanent loss would be was debated and unclear. There were various opinions.

On this premise, it seemed best to some to wait until the age of volatility gave way to moral stability. Since it was agreed to by all that this was in fact entry into salvation, they considered it wiser to pass through adolescence and early life, into stable adulthood, before entering. This would to them serve as a safeguard in case they went a bit wild in those years.

The other side argued that baptism itself, the regeneration, would serve as the protection, along with guidance of the home and Christian community, to prevent such from ever occurring in the first place. This side ultimately won and was re-established as the only acceptable Christian norm until the Reformation period about a thousand years later.

My takeaway was pretty simple: this was no mere outward profession: this was in fact a salvific act. And such a belief is profoundly central. I mean, we are talking about the very means of entry into this early (and enduring) community. Not one source could I find to argue against its efficacy prior to the Reformation.

Communion

What was it? Was it merely a "symbol" (as we now use the term) to help us "remember" (again, as we use the term) some past salvific act of Christ? Was it merely crackers and grape juice as I was taught? Or was it an actual participation in the person of Christ, physically? Was it in fact His Body and Blood (John 6:50-58)? [11]

Again, I found a universal voice. It was His body and blood. While some in the early writings used the term "symbol," the Greek term σύμβολον appeared to have a different meaning. It meant to "throw together," as in "the physical and the spiritual" together, like the Incarnation itself, in stark contrast to the idea of "separate, but representing." Not one source I found argued against the belief this was in fact the Body and Blood of Christ, excepting the Gnostics, who refused it because they rejected His material existence, claiming he only appeared to be physical.

And again, the impossibility of the Church being divided over the meaning and reality of the exact central focal point of the assembling together with *no* record of such a profound controversy, the idea that the Apostles left any room for ambiguity over the central ritual of the faith being a ridiculous take on church history, was stark.

Salvation

What was it? Was it something to be obtained through faith at an altar call as I was taught, held as a commodity so long as one didn't turn apostate through denying belief in Christ? Was it a legal transaction in which Christ was punished by the Father for

---

[11] In fact, this is the only place I've seen in the New Testament which incorporates both, "Amen, amen" and, "*Alithos,*"meaning actually and truly, to emphasize a point.

crimes He never committed, leaving us pardoned for all past and future crimes, regardless of our ensuing actions? Was it obtained by believing and confessing only? Or was it a process, a relationship of trust and actions, begun at baptism (or even before as the Spirit led us to Christ) and continuing until death, never to be presumed upon in this life, but rather being pled for in a continuous prayer of "Lord Jesus Christ, Son of God, have mercy on me, a sinner?"[12]

Again, the latter proved to be the case.

It was at this point that I realized I could not in good conscience return to Protestantism, although if you removed the *solas* Lutherans were fairly close. Only there is no real Lutheranism without the *solas*.[13] Yet on the other hand, I could not go forward to Orthodoxy. You see, the icons were obviously idolatry, the intercessions of the Saints were clearly necromancy, and the priests were unashamed added mediators between men and God.

---

[12] I had begun to do a pass through the New Testament collecting passages which told us how to be saved, acquire the Kingdom, obtain a favorable Judgment, etc., which were essentially synonyms. After pages and pages of citations, I never completed it. I invite the reader to do so, as a test whether salvation "by faith alone" is truly the Christian message conveyed in scripture.

[13] The *solas* here refer to the five solae of the Protestant Reformation: Christians are saved by grace alone (*Sola gratia*), through faith alone (*Sola fide*), in Christ alone (*solus Christus*), as revealed by Scripture alone (*sola Scriptura*), to the glory of God alone (*soli Deo gloria*).

Chapter 6

"Lead us throughout the way into Your Kingdom."

I wish there was some way to convey the torment of this period of near-hopelessness for Anastasia and me (she had traveled every step of this journey beside me, as I reported each finding to her. We were in this together from day one to the baptistry to this very day).

Without exaggeration, there were many mornings in which we awoke in horror. Had we become apostates? Had we cut ourselves off? Here we were trying to be honest and sincere, in all diligence, pursuing an understanding of God, and left with nothing. Like following a marker in the sky while rowing a boat, only to find ourselves too far from land to return, no land in sight ahead, and the marker seeming to vanish as thick, dark clouds rolled in, not knowing if they'd ever pass on by. Truly lost. I wish I could convey the trepidation of this process to an Orthodox person who was born and raised in the church and takes their faith or granted.

On a short visit to the nearby monastery, I discussed my turmoil with a wonderful, warm monk. He told me that morning he had just read the passage of the Apostles being out on the boat in the storm. He reminded me how, when Jesus stepped on the boat, they were immediately at the shore, and I would find myself there suddenly and unexpectedly as well. While this was little more than was a bit comforting to me at the time, when my "suddenly" happened in the near future, I remembered his words.

On those frequent mornings of terror, I would talk myself down: "Yes, this stuff is wrong. But if it's so wrong as to make those who practice and believe it no longer Christians, then the Church ceased to exist for about fifteen hundred years. And Jesus said the gates of hell would never prevail against it (Matthew 16:18)," was my usual argument made to myself in order to calm my anxieties.

Among the many people I consulted, two had the most profound impact.

The first was a Greek Orthodox priest named Fr. Steve, who served at a parish with an unusually large number of converts. I met him at a small gathering of Catholic and Orthodox clergy to which Anastasia and I had been invited by Fr. Daniel, which discussed the question of catechesis. Following the Christianization of known world, the need to catechize converts fell away, as most people were simply born into the faith. Later, as the West expanded into new lands, came a need to instruct new adult believers. The Catholics looked back into earlier times for guidance in reviving the practice, and the main speaker was a Catholic priest who shared their history as a template for the Orthodox (bottom line: what you need is almost always available in church history).

At the break, sitting at a table with Fr. Steve, I explained my dilemma. From what I'd found, the use of icons, intercessions of the saints, and a couple other practices were not what they seemed to start out being in the earlier years of the Church (there is an implied understanding among most Protestants that the Apostles laid out and handed down everything, complete, from the beginning; every change or addition was "from men," and therefore wrong).

His response: "Neither is the Bible [what it started out as being]."

Remember that this was what got me into this mess? The formation of the canon? Those few words hit me like a ton of bricks. He was right. These letters of personal correspondence were not "the canon of scripture" back then. That was only codified some three hundred years later. In fact, for decades there was literally no written instruction. No epistles. And as each one was written, it took some time to copy and disseminate to the other churches, some not having all of them for quite a long time. It was a development of understanding and usage of something which itself took some time to produce in the first place.

Was there in fact a period of general development in which the Church came to begin, discover, unfold, and solidify a number of things together? I was now open to the possibility that this all happened over those few early centuries. Yet the fact that one thing (the Bible) clearly did develop, which I knew to be correct in its final state, did not necessitate that they all were of that same divine source. These others still could have been aberrations. So at least the idea of later formation of its current state was no longer a "deal breaker" in itself. Nonetheless, I did acknowledge that my trust in this Bible inferred my trust in the fidelity of the Christians over the first several hundred years. If I couldn't trust them, how could I trust the book they handed me? I was already taking their word for authorship and unaltered preservation of the original texts. Quite the quandary.

So, the seemingly unanswerable question remained: were these things of men or of God? And how on earth could I know? Against what would I measure to find out? Myself? No. I had already begun by acknowledging the inadequacy of my own individual judgments. So now what?

Enter Abouna Bishoy Brownfield. The American convert Coptic Orthodox priest (one of only a few in the world).

You do not simply meet Abouna Bishoy. You experience him. A relatively unknown legend. No cell phone, no internet. No traveling to speak at other parishes. Yet to those who know him, a truly profound and impressive figure. Legendary is no exaggeration.

Meeting for the first time at an outdoor café, across from me sat an older, very white, slightly rounded yet solid, stout man who was every bit as American as I. He had a long white beard, deep and authoritative voice, and had grown up only a handful of miles from my hometown, both being very similar communities. He had been a body builder, something of a gearhead (fast car enthusiast), had owned a gym, and later became an editor of a body building magazine. He met an Egyptian woman, converted, married, and pursued this form of spirituality with a vigor seldom seen anywhere. To this day I've never met a more well-read or more well-spoken man. His demeanor was sober, profound and serious, or else loose and gruff with humor, and not too much in between. I had grown up with music, movies, TV shows, and friends which predated me, so his being more than fifteen years my senior posed no barrier to our cultural connection. In fact, to this day, we spend time talking on occasion and are almost always on the exact same page in our shared yet separate histories as (now) older Southern California Americans.

To the Copts, he was, "more Coptic than we are!" Stern and unyielding, he transferred the extraordinary self-disciplines involved in being a competitive body builder many years prior to his Coptic spiritual life (indeed he had at one point been a Junior Mr. Olympia), which is likewise heavy on self-control. While explaining to me how his being a mystagogue at heart was the impetus for him pursuing and flourishing in this church upon encountering it, the dovetailing of one who spent a life demanding the obedience of his body to his mind with the ascetic practices of Coptic Orthodoxy seemed to me to have been a natural fit.

After explaining my journey to this point, I presented him with my conundrum: "I have no way to determine if these later developments are from men or from God."

"They're from men. *Pause.* Men with God in them," was his deep-voiced simple, yet profound reply, as if this was the dumbest question he'd ever heard. That was it. And those few words rocked me back in my seat. It was like a giant light bulb went on. That man has an uncanny ability to sum things up in a single line or two.

"I had been asking a question which was based on an Old Testament paradigm!"

Throughout this journey, various Orthodox had said things to me like, "You don't understand the Incarnation," and, "It's the Church." And it just didn't resonate. Until now.

It was like in a moment it all flooded my mind at once.

I had come to understand soteriology through an Orthodox lens—at least in an intellectual sense—in which salvation was not entirely about one event, the legal satisfaction being obtained at the cross, but about everything. The bigger picture was that of a separation between God and man being bridged in a very real ontological sense (the very real state of our being) through uniting the very divinity of God with fallen human personhood, in all its aspects, excepting sin. This process of unification (and thus restoring and healing) began in the largest sense (though in another sense you can trace it back through the prophets and everything He did since the Fall of man) at the Incarnation. This was the moment of union. Real union. Healing us by uniting us with Himself. Becoming man. The concept of exchange. He taking what is ours and giving us what is His, in Himself, is the most prominent soteriological theme in Orthodoxy.

Until this time, man was not truly united to God. Man had always been separated, with the Spirit falling on or visiting them, and not really *dwelling in* them in this ontological sense. This union was the entire point of salvation history. And beginning that very real union of being by taking flesh from Saint Mary, fulfilling all things truly human throughout the course of His life, teaching us what it means to properly be human, suffering for us, taking our death and overcoming it, the completion of this union was in His taking us in Himself and sitting down in Heaven at the right hand of the Father.

The Church became His Body. God now dwelt in man, and man in God.

I finally saw the Church.

Although I have been (rightly) accused of arrogance at times, such arrogance couldn't be made to extend to the notion that every person in whom the Spirit dwelt misunderstood these basic tenets of the faith, or was blindly unaware of radical deviations, yet I (or insert any historical figure such as those at the time of the Reformation or the thousands of schisms since) had some special measure of the Spirit, or intelligence, or sincerity or piety to finally understand that Voice. Certainly, the Protestant "scholars" of the last five hundred years weren't privy to some linguistic or contextual understanding which the early Christian Fathers lacked. I mean, they literally still lived in the context of the writings, spoke the language and oversaw the communities in which the teachings and practices were handed down.

Moreover, all these things I had questioned not only became accepted practices only by virtue of the people of God affirming them, they stood as right and necessary due to this union based on its bare implications. I had never realized the deep misanthropy, not dissimilar to early Gnostic thought, in my former beliefs. I had considered anything "from man" as inherently wrong. But it was not, at least not by its human origins in itself.

One's epistemological disposition (how one determines what is true) directs one where to turn for answers and guidance and to discern right from wrong, grey areas from boundaries. Will that guide be self or will it be the voice of two thousand years? Are there precedents to inform and shape our view, or are we indeed unencumbered innovators of new religion? For me, I now had those answers. Listen to the voice of the Church.

I was finally home.

Chapter 7

"...the one holy, catholic, and apostolic Church"

Now to back up and run the parallel story of subjective experience with the Copts that I promised earlier. The story of conversion, from encountering the early church to embracing Orthodoxy as her continued, truest expression, was that of an intellectual journey. Yet there was also a personal and experiential one. Although concurrent, there was a very real distinction between the two.

So now, the other half of that journey of inquiry.

Following my encounter with Saint Irenaeus, and my decision to go back to the writings of the early church to obtain their beliefs, I decided to check out one of those early churches in person at the same time. Throughout my minimal encounter with the early church in the canon study, one city stood out: Alexandria. This was the intellectual capital of the Roman Empire, and played a central role in the formation of many aspects of the church in the early centuries. Certainly Saint Athanasius, with his epithet *Contra mundum*, or against the world, which he received as he opposed the heresy of Arius, even when he was a deacon offering the primary term of the "same essence as the Father" to understand the relationship of Christ with the Father, left a significant impact on me.

And so, it happened that I knew of this huge building in a nearby town, which I understand some locals to mistake for a mosque due to the massive dome. The large lettering on the wall on the street side of the structure read "See of Alexandria."[14] I decided this was the place to begin.

Knowing nothing about the Coptic Orthodox (indeed, at this point in life I had never even knowingly met one), and worse yet being of German upbringing, I showed up early on Sunday morning, before the liturgy began. I didn't realize it at the time, and the significance wouldn't even hit me for years, but it was the Sunday of the Prodigal Son during Lent. I found someone inside, told them why I was there, and was told, "Talk to Father Daniel. He's the young priest with the black beard." (The other priests were older and he was pretty new). Since he hadn't arrived yet, I went back outside to the steps which led up to the large wooden doors adorned with crosses to wait. There was no mistaking him as he approached. The long black dress (as I saw it anyway), the large cross hanging on his neck, and the black beard told me this was the guy. He walked up to me, a tattoo sleeved biker wearing jeans and a white tee shirt, I suppose he guessed me to be the owner of the Harley in the parking lot, with a warm and welcoming smile, thankfully. Though I smiled back politely, I was there on business.

I briefly explained to him how I got there, my introduction to church history, and my intent to learn more about the Orthodox.

Abouna Daniel said, "Well, stick around a while and see how you like it."

I replied, "How I like it is utterly irrelevant. If I love it and it's not true, I'm leaving. And if I hate it but it is true, I need to conform to it."

---

[14] The funny thing is had this not been there, had it merely said "Coptic" or "American Coptic" as is common now, I'd never have looked twice.

While likely not the most respectful reply in retrospect, it did reflect some basic truths on which I had landed as an Evangelical Christian. While decorum already wasn't my strong suit (not that I didn't know how, I just stopped caring as much over the years), my being on a quest for God and truth, I was probably more zealous and even less conscious of social niceties than usual. This was, after all, a quest for the ultimate of all truths, and social etiquette was the last thing on my mind.

Living in the world of consumerist Christianity, heavy on customer satisfaction and emotional resonance epistemology, it had become clear to me that choosing one's beliefs based on personal preference at the open buffet court of local churches and online preachers was indeed to construct a god in one's own image. I had recognized this self-worship as the standard American consumerist path and had no interest in it. A mirror seemed a rather precarious place to worship. What happens at the end? Who will save me if I've been worshiping myself?[15]

No, what I like had to be set aside. This was a truth quest.

Additionally, it had seemed clear to my wife and I, and indeed to a number of like-minded friends, that the idea of self-sacrifice and self-denial were conspicuously absent in this market-driven, personality-oriented self-help Western religion, whose "practical" teachings were often little more than a redirection of those seeking heaven back down towards the earth and this transient life. This stood in stark juxtaposition to the

---

[15] In my experience, the overwhelming majority of people never really think about these things in any questioning or challenging way. They tend to be good-hearted and sincere folks who simply presume what is being told to them has been checked out and verified by others. And that includes most people from most faiths. The intents are usually good while the scrutiny is lacking.

cross as a symbol of the faith. Such attention to a fulfilling life here on earth was not only absent in the early writings I would soon encounter, but was the utter antithesis of the ethos of that early Church of which I was just becoming aware. Yet within its own theological structure it made sense. The cross was His, which He bore in order that we should not need to, leaving us with only the upside of things, in a sense. He paid, but we walk off with the goods. Heaven has already been secured by a prayer at an altar call. What was left then to obtain? Only earth. And maybe some extra special rewards in Heaven for those willing to sacrifice for them through service and moral improvements.

One can see the appeal of such a message, especially to a consumerist society. Market researched data and team meetings centered around presenting superior customer service, instructing servants when to cheer and applaud, continuously needing to change programs and songs so things don't become stale, and constant hyping—all these things had become rather distasteful to Anastasia and I as we sought something more profound. Indeed, this is a common story among Evangelicals who convert to older forms of the faith.

Walking into the liturgy after our brief introduction on the steps, a few things hit me hard. Nobody greeted me. Nobody really even looked at me. There was nobody on a stage facing me. It was as if they didn't even notice I had arrived. The lecterns were off to the sides. Standing center, elevated, was the altar. All eyes were facing it, rather than facing me. In my prior experience I was always the center of attention, being the consumer. From the friendly and helpful parking lot guides, to the warm and welcoming greeters at the doors, to the ushers inside, to the upbeat worship team, to the popular pastor on the stage, everything had been directed towards me.

"Wait! I'm not a customer here??? God takes the center position? Even when they give the sermon, they remain off to the side while He remains center??? *What?*"

I cannot begin to express how right this felt, at least in this regard. As is the case with many sincere Evangelicals who find their religion rather vacuous, as if there is something profound and solemn missing, I instinctively knew why things were arranged as they were. I knew why even when he gave the homily he remained to the side, not walking back and forth in order to connect with the congregation as one would see on a stage with a stand-up comic, a motivational speaker, or a timeshare salesman. This place was holy; nothing was arranged as it was for stylistic, fashionable reasons. Indeed, I soon learned that even the colors, building arrangement, and materials had meaning, rather than being the result of a marketing team, a pastor's wife, and a decorator with swatches.

As I stood in a pew in the back, someone came to help me, opening one of the liturgy books and helping me to follow along. Thank God![16]

While the icon and kissing the hand of the priest with a few other things presented what I believed were impenetrable barriers, I quickly decided that I would remain awhile, seeing what good things I could gather to take back with me when I returned to the Evangelical world. There was admittedly some sense of relief in having settled the matter of permanence so quickly. Knowing this was a temporary learning and gathering

---

[16] While I hear many complaints about how alienating an ethnic Coptic parish can be, and there is some truth there which I will address later. I can say that in my experience, and the next week when my wife joined me, it only took one person—one—to make me feel welcomed and remove that sense of being lost.

endeavor alleviated some pressures I sensed regarding a necessary future decision.

The liturgy was *so* long! I can say in all honesty that I didn't have much inward experience which I could sense. And such was the case throughout many, if not most liturgies. Maybe I'm just not the "type," since I didn't get all emotional during the romantic worship songs and jumping up and down with the hand waving at my Evangelical churches either, as many around me were visibly moved, and many women often crying. I suppose I'm just not too emotional; I think I'm okay with that. And at the very least I can say there is just a sense of dishonesty I know I would feel if I tried to conjure up inward experience anyway. Integrity is a big thing for me.

Yet something strange was happening of which I was unaware in the moment. There came afterwards, when I left, a sense of peace, which I did not notice much but was very apparent to Anastasia. And as I returned each week it continued, again unbeknownst to me, yet increasingly noticeable to my family and those in the repair shop I managed. It was not until they pointed it out that I even noticed the extent of the change. It seems even my speech wasn't peppered with F-bombs every fourth word, as had been my custom.

At my prior Evangelical churches, the service began with an upbeat happy-clappy fun-time song, moved through a bit slower one, and landed on a slow tune with a standard deep slow drumbeat accompanying the repetition of a few words over and over, the lyrics being apparently inspired by the desperate love of a teenager for her boyfriend, as I heard it described by some of my Protestant friends of older and more sober denominations. This culminated in a sermon designed to make you feel more positive about your life and how to navigate it more successfully, and that high lasted all the way to the parking lot, at which point it evaporated when someone cut you off and inspired a finger in response.

Yet here it was the opposite.

The service was slow and arduous. Certainly, even the chanting style in no way resonated with my Western ear (I'm sorry to say that it largely doesn't to this day. Again, just something about my wiring doesn't match). It generally was accompanied after short time by a backache. And it went on forever, it seemed. Yet the peace, which was not an emotional high, seemed to arrive afterwards, and remained for days. Later on, when I began praying the *Agpeya*, the Book of Hours, which is a book of recited prayers, the same thing occurred. Long and boring initially, yet a peace following later which endured. So also this peace seemed to arrive and remain each time I sat with Abouna Daniel to ask questions and chat. And later on, with virtually all clergy I met.

Two weeks after walking into a Coptic Church for the first time, I lost my job of twenty-eight years. I won't go into what happened, but it was sudden, unexpected and very ugly. I will add that lies and dishonesty were involved, as well as some bad judgment on my part. What was worse, we lived on the lot where I worked, so we lost our place to live as well. I can't describe the shock and devastation, but I knew this was no coincidence. Something spiritual was at play, directing things, but I had no idea who was doing what. I only knew this was not merely the happenstances of life, and something here was either very right, and dark spiritual forces were trying to stop it, or very wrong, and God was doing something in response. I have come to conclude neither was totally correct. Without being so presumptuous as to claim to truly understand the complexities of happenings in the heavenlies, I can say that the ensuing events and time on unemployment (having worked without much break even for vacations since the age of sixteen, and the government having extended the unemployment period to two years, I decided to take some time off to ride my motorcycle and live for a while as I chose) gave me the free time to dig in and research the things I was hearing, as well as attend the midweek liturgies frequently. I couldn't begin to count the hours I spent on this, as well as learning to practice the spiritual disciplines I was learning (like the prayer rule).

Overall, there were maybe four or so people who helped us during the liturgy over the first weeks, standing with us and showing us where we were in the book, while also explaining the meanings of some things we were seeing. They were sufficient to make us feel welcomed and less disoriented. In time, as I was in my own mind gathering some good things to take with me when I left, the first profound practice I undertook was making the sign of the cross.

Having found it recorded by Tertullian around 200 AD,[17] knowing the practice predated this writing significantly (such is generally the case when we see written mention of a practice), and seeing it enduring through about two millennia, finding no adequate answer to the question, "Why did we stop doing this?" but rather concluding it to have been a knee-jerk negative reaction to the Catholics by the Western Reformers (indeed, I came to discover many deletions to be the result of this "Romophobia"), I decided to give it a try.

I had a Labrador. A black one. Schatzi. A purebred. I got her for half price from the pet store because she had outgrown the

---

[17] Tertullian, *De corona (The Chaplet)*, 3.

cage. She was extremely skittish from this extended period of confinement. One day I took her to a lake and found out she was terrified of the water. I thought to myself, "You're a Labrador! Water is in your soul! What's wrong with you?!" I later took her to a small pond, this time in my shorts, ready for a swim. I went in first. I swam out to the middle and called for her. Panting and hopping on the shore because she couldn't get to her master, she jumped in and swam to me. You could actually see the fear turn to confidence within a few feet as she began to paddle. From that day on she loved water. She just had to enter in in order to discover who she had been all along. After that day, I could sit on a shore and toss a tennis ball out in a lake, or even the ocean, and off she would fly to retrieve it fearlessly.

That is how it felt for me the first time I made the sign of the cross on myself. It was like something in me knew I was designed for this. And so it was with a number of things. Yet I intentionally was setting all the experiential evidences on a shelf, so to speak, trying my best to stick to my objective tests for the authentic Christian faith practiced from the beginning. I could (and indeed would) go back to these experiences later to sort and file them in light of the truths I'd find once the objective testing was finished. And so, on I continued with my catechesis and liturgies.

Once I passed through the barriers mentioned earlier (icons, intercessions, etc.) and it seemed I was now at peace with this, Abouna Daniel mentioned the word *baptism*. When we got home, Anastasia and I discussed our mutual terror. She said she finally understood what it was like for a man who was dating and the girl said, "We should get married." Sure, there were things you couldn't do (like taking communion), but why ruin a good thing?

In Evangelicalism, a church was like a girlfriend. You have a fight and you break up. You go find a new one down the block.

No commitment needed. And there is all manner of type and looks from which to choose. Moreover, none would reject you. Better than dating. Heck, they did not even care about your past!

But this was marriage. And not even like American marriage. This was for life! No turning back. My wife has often quipped about marriage here in the West, "They're like pancakes. You throw the first one out." Such perception of permanence and the ramifications of leaving were not even spoken explicitly to us, but rather it was clear in everything we had learned and read, and inherent in the lengthy (a year minimum is a fairly wise and common standard) catechesis. Nobody had to say it. This is no doubt why Jesus warned us to count the cost before making the decision to become a disciple, which stands in stark juxtaposition to the Evangelical altar call which follows a forty-minute sermon. Imagine your daughter met a guy an hour and a half ago and announces she is marrying him today. And which is the more important and profound commitment: marriage or Christ? It took some time to settle into this idea. One major consideration was if we moved one day? What if Abouna Daniel moved or was not available anymore? Could we remain? This had to be settled before the decision could be made.

Among the earliest impacting experiences in the Coptic Orthodox Church for both of us was the "flavor" similarity between these people and the early Church about which we had always read in the New Testament. Something in the demeanor, culture, and spiritual posture just seemed to fit precisely into the picture we had previously formed mentally about these earliest Christians. Or perhaps as we experienced this community, the things we read came to light in a way that they hadn't before. Probably more like the two just fit together because they were the same.

As we soon discovered this was no fluke. The early Church was a small Middle Eastern persecuted religious minority community. The Copts had more or less, not by their own choosing, remained in this scenario and culture continuously throughout almost all of their existence. While I couldn't name what it was specifically about them that gave off this aroma of the early Church for the longest time, it was palpably present.

Having visited a couple other Orthodox jurisdictions, the ethos of the people wasn't the same. Similar, but a little different. And yes, I am biased as I write this.[18]

Most folks in America choose the church that fits with them, just as they also choose from the variety of offerings in almost every aspect of life: from food to clothing to cars to everything. I did rather the opposite. Intentionally.

My thinking was that I didn't need more of what I had the most already, but more of what I lacked the most. And this community, being very much my opposite, had in abundance what I had the least. If the goal was the healing of my broken and fallen state, I'd need to work out the most damaged and weakest areas in me as a priority. They majored where I minored.

Eventually, I felt I had put my finger on it: the kissing of both sides of the hands.

When the word "thanks" or "thanksgiving" is spoken in prayer (including the liturgy, which itself is really one long prayer), Copts kiss the fronts and backs of the hands. This means,

---

[18] I have come to conclude that each cultural jurisdiction has its own majors and minors. None being superior overall, but each having a unique flavor. And each emphasized trait has its own pros and cons, likely being formed by unique cultural experiences. I have also noted that the Copts tend to have more exposure to the wonderful minds and luminaries of the Eastern Orthodox than the reverse. This I consider a plus as well.

"we are thankful for what we receive and what we don't receive, the good and the bad," which is to say "we accept all things as if they come from God for our salvation." This humble submission and mindfulness of the presence of God in all things is the very core of the common ethos. In fact, to my awareness, the Copts alone have a specific Thanksgiving Prayer, which always follows the Lord's Prayer in the daily prayers and at beginning parts of the liturgy. In it is prayed: "We thank You for every condition, concerning every condition. and in whatever condition."

I, as a six foot, two hundred forty-pound, tattoo sleeved American biker, had power. Power face to face. Power with legal recourse, both civil and criminal. I was certainly nobody's victim. But they did not have such power or recourse throughout most of their history in Egypt.

Coming from a land and history in which they were a small minority, with an often times hostile surrounding religious culture and virtually non-exist system of true legal protections, their day-to-day, hour-to-hour reliance on God was simply life as it was known. Their life is that of a simple and deep faith, clinging to God. The joy over the rewards of martyrdom stretched back to the early centuries of the church, during which Egypt was often a prime target for hostile emperors. Few things could be more mismatched than the Copts and I.

There is a saying that when the scientists ascend to the top of the last mountain of knowledge, they will find the theologian sitting there. To which I would add that when the theologians ascend their last mountain, they will find an old illiterate Egyptian woman sitting in front of an icon.

Incidentally, my intellectually and apologetically inclined nature, coming from an older Western paradigm (as opposed to the more recent emotionally and experientially inclined post-modern Western thought, in which feelings are equated to knowledge), seems to have inadvertently placed me in a position of possessing some things of value which they largely lacked. While they sensed many things intuitively, felt things inwardly, and viewed things through the less-than-precise lens of their ethos, I was different. I systematized, ordered and articulated things in a logical and structured manner. So it seems what I had was of some value to them as well.

Go figure.

In any case, this seemed the most well-suited community to help me with my salvation (while some Copts have voiced their disapproval with the rate of growth of this somewhat gruff and at times rude blue collar American outsider, for which I do apologize and plead for patience, I can say that the overwhelming majority of them, elder and younger alike, have been more than welcoming and warm.)

We were baptized, chrismated, married, and communed on Easter night, following an early Christian custom. I took the name Irenaeus, Michelle was given (her new name revealed at baptism as chosen by Abouna Daniel) the name Anastasia, after the Resurrection (as opposed to the saint). Having done a full catechesis, a full Lent, several services a week, attending almost all of the Holy Week services, following over a year of intensive studies, it is hard to describe how impacting the night truly was. As we walked with candles, dressed in white, at the rear of the procession, the people of Saint John parish who witnessed the long process all seemed to smile as we passed, which is not common at a Coptic Orthodox liturgy. We had entered the community.

Being at a fairly ethnic parish, especially at midweek liturgies, the elders had begun by looking at me with suspicion. But this was understandable.

Having grown up with hostile outsiders all around them, having seen Protestants come peeling off members for centuries trying to "save" them, and being a small minority again in a post-9/11 America who knew of no difference between a Copt and a Muslim, they tended to huddle together for safety and a sense of familiarity. Surely, I seemed as out of place, rolling up on my Harley Davidson wearing jeans and a tee shirt as any Egyptian grandmother would walking into a biker bar. I can't sufficiently emphasize how important it was for me to extend grace toward those who feared me.

Pro tip: walking in with my head down, not looking at faces with a smile hoping for reciprocation, but looking at the floor and/or icons, paying attention to the liturgy, and maintaining the posture and demeanor of an outsider seemed the best way to assimilate, or at least not alienate myself more than is expected, which is really just a form of humility, which is the prime virtue of these people.

So often I hear complaints about the exclusivity of the ethnic parishes, yet I seldom hear a call for understanding of their fears and concerns. And these have been validated to my mind by instances I've seen of American converts in their new home (this is rare, but more common among the marry-in converts and their spouses, for whom social acceptance seems much more important, and is well-intentioned), at times wanting to assuage the sense of alienation by importing aspects of their culture or former religion into the ethnic parishes. There is a balance and some guidelines to all this that I'll cover later. I don't really have a side in this tension so much as some basic considerations and boundaries I feel to be useful.

After a couple of years however, something happened. Something unexpected.

The old Coptic women, those old stone-faced angry looking ones (I figured out after a while that the lack of smiling in the church was not a sign of a lack of joy, but a solemnity and a humility in the House of Angels), began smiling at me (after liturgy). This was a shock. Totally unexpected.

I still don't know whether it was seeing me at midweek liturgies (almost all Arabic) multiple times a week during Lent, or reports of my zeal to embrace and perpetuate the Coptic ethos and traditions at youth meetings with their grandkids, or what. But suddenly they began smiling at me. Keep in mind, I never saw them smile at anyone—not even each other!

While I came for God, and if nobody had ever smiled at me it wouldn't have deterred my pursuit since I was truly convinced that He was present, and since their deep ethos was for the most part absorbed through mere presence, simply being allowed to pray with them was enough. I never came for a social club.

While not sought or expected, I can say in all sincerity that those smiles meant more to me than all the warm embraces by all the Evangelical greeters before. To this day I feel no sense of alienation or trepidation walking into any new Coptic parish anywhere.

Thilo Young

My mother, Marguerita (Omi) Cadle, in Germany and England.

My American Flight to Egypt

Miguel Hernandez, my paternal grandfather.

From left to right: my maternal grandmother Margarethe (Oma), me, my paternal grandmother Victoria (Nana), and my uncle Ernie.

From left to right: my brother Lloyd, me, and my sister Klaudia in El Monte.

Jesus (Jesse): First Holy Communion (left), and in El Monte showering under the garden hose on a hot day (right).

Thilo and Michelle, Wedding in Venice Beach, California.

Baptism, 2012

Ordination, Reader

Parish life

A long liturgy

Part II: Anastasia's Story

Chapter 8

*Train up a child in the way he should go: and when
he is old, he will not depart from it.
Proverbs 22:6*

It was Saturday evening, April 14, 2012. I stood with my bare feet on the cold tile in the narthex at Saint John Coptic Orthodox Church in West Covina, California. My priest (Abouna), Daniel Habib stood before me. I was not yet sure if I wanted to cry in joy or throw up from fear.

Abouna Daniel gently smiled and asked, "Do you want to know your baptism name?" While most adult converts choose their own baptism name, I thought it more appropriate that my spiritual father who in the past year had come to know me so well and knew all the saints, be the one to name his newest spiritual daughter. It was my idea that he choose my name, but it was his idea to make me wait until my baptism day to reveal the surprise. I could hardly wait. "Yes," I said with excitement. He paused for a moment then said, "Anastasia." In that moment, time stood still. It was that space where it is just you and God and all else disappears. I would later come to learn that the fathers call this timeless-time, *Kairos*.

"Anastasia."

The name floated in the air and it was as if I heard it from Creator's own mouth. I was overwhelmed by the beauty of the name alone, but then Abouna Daniel added, "It means *resurrection*."

Resurrection. A whole new life. Could it be? Was it possible? There was so much death I needed to be resurrected from and so much of my own sin and corruption that needed redemption. Lost in Kairos, my heart ached with a bright-sadness as my mind began to embrace this promise of a new beginning.

I grew up in a little suburban community, in a time and place where one could allow their five-year-old to walk alone a block away to take herself to church. And that is exactly what my family did. They were not particularly religious, rather quite the opposite. There was darkness and violence one wouldn't wish on their worst enemy. And religion? Horoscopes and palm-reading were preferable over the white-washed world of church-goers. However, Sunday School was a good way to get an energetic little girl out of the way for a while and my family was all for that.

The church I attended was a small Non-denominational/Evangelical congregation. For my Orthodox friends, that sounds like a mouthful, but you will discover the distinctive title to be essential to the context of my long journey. A lot occurred in my life between the ages of 5 and 13. Most of it bad. It involved physical, mental, and sexual abuse. Even religious abuse. The holy and precious Name of God would be used to shame me or to keep me in line. One example I would often hear, "Many are called but few are chosen" (Matthew 22:14). This passage would be used as a reminder that there were a lot of good, godly people in the world, but I was fooling myself if I thought I was one of them. The belief that I was unloved and unlovable was set firmly in stone during these formative years. This would prove to be not only a stumbling block in my relationship with the Lord, but also fertile ground in which bad doctrine would flourish.

All glory to God, He never left me entirely alone. My mother married a kind and gentle man when I was around 13 years old. Shortly after, I visited my new extended family in Dallas, Pennsylvania, including the sweetest little white-haired Baptist grandma. She was everything you imagine in an old-fashioned grandma with her gentle spirit, and what a cook! But do not let her sweetness fool you. When it came to matters of her dedication to the Lord through firm adherence to her Baptist beliefs, she was tenacious.

During our visit, she inquired if I had ever asked Jesus into my heart. Though I had attended church since I was five, I had no recollection of such an event. My response of "no" provoked from her an expression of great concern. She spoke to me gently but emphatically, stating that until that time when we formally renounce our sins and ask Jesus into our heart to be our Lord and Savior—even if we grow up in a Christian home and go to church our entire life—we are not saved.

This did not seem to fit with the closeness I had experienced with God when reading the Bible or in my times of prayer or singing songs to Him. Still, she warned me of *counterfeit* Christianity, where the devil makes us *feel* like we are saved but we are not. The scariest part is we would not even discover the deception until the time of Judgment when Jesus says the shocking statement, "Depart from Me for I never knew you." I was terrified.

Please forgive me as I pause for a moment to explain the use of the term "counterfeit Christianity" and how it is used within many Protestant denominations. This sidetrack is important as my hope is, at the same time of sharing my journey, to offer the reader a greater understanding of Protestant beliefs. I pray this might equip the Coptic community to better share their faith with Protestant friends and family.

So what is "counterfeit Christianity?" Many Protestant denominations believe, "Once saved, always saved." This belief is two-fold: the first is that salvation is a transaction; Your part is that you repent and ask Jesus into your heart. His part is that He extends the payment He made on the cross to cover your debt. Whether or not this transaction occurs determines if you are going to heaven or going to hell. The second is that, once you've asked Jesus into your heart, none of your works—neither good nor bad—can affect your final destination.

If you're wondering to yourself how no works are involved if you have to ask Jesus into your heart, which is clearly doing something, therefore a "work," believe me, that has been an argument within the Protestant community for years. The differing proposed solutions have been the cause of many new splinters in the Protestant family tree—but we will leave that alone for now.

All of this to say, the general belief is, if you prayed the right formula, and believe me the *right* formula is critical, and sincerely meant it, your passport to heaven has been stamped and there's no changing it.

Of course, one cannot deny how many people fall away from the faith, as our Lord's parable of the Sower reveals, so to reconcile the reality that people walk away from God with the teaching that you do not have the ability to walk away from God, the solution is—you guessed it—the conversion had to be counterfeit Christianity: Meaning the person only *thought* they were saved, but were in fact only deceived and weren't as sincere when they prayed as they felt they were. I can tell you to this day that most Protestant Evangelicals who have been in the faith for a while, admit that they have prayed this prayer a repeatedly—either out of fear that the first time may not have been sincere enough—or just as a "just in case," back up.

Of course, frightened of such a potential outcome, I quickly asked my grandmother to help me to pray the correct formula, known as The Sinner's Prayer. I prayed, "Lord Jesus Christ, I am a sinner. Please forgive me and come into my heart."

When I concluded the prayer, I was a little confused and empty because I did not feel any different, so I was not sure if my prayer had worked. My grandma, with great joy, assured me that *now* my name was written in the Lamb's Book of Life and all the angels were rejoicing.

Though in that moment I was greatly relieved, this teaching that I might be deceived into thinking I was saved from hell, would prove to cause me much inner turmoil for decades to come.

When I came home from my visit to Pennsylvania, I decided to be baptized. In the non-denominational/Evangelical tradition, baptism was encouraged, but not mandatory. It is viewed as merely an "outward profession of an inward decision." Much like how wearing a wedding ring is not what makes one married, but we do it to declare to the world that we love and belong to someone.

Of course, this loose view would have curled my Baptist grandmother's toes, as in her tradition, baptism is *quite* mandatory to be saved from hell. Regardless of denomination vs. denomination, now that I was officially "saved," I wanted to take what I believed to be the next right steps. So in 1982, on some non-descript midweek day, I went with a couple of family members to my little church. It was not much of an event. A few of the church administrative staff were pulled away from their desks to serve as witnesses. I waded down into the baptismal font at the front of the empty little church. The associate pastor's voice echoed in the empty room as he asked me for my confession.

"Do you believe that Jesus is the Christ and that He died for your sins?"

"Yes."

"Upon that confession of faith, I now baptize you in the name of the Father, the Son, and the Holy Spirit."

Once again, I emerged not feeling much different than before, but I was now assured by at least two denominations of Protestantism that I was as good as in.[19]

---

[19] I pray the reader is beginning to pick up on the significant nuances of the estimated more than 45,000 Protestant denominations, as again, this will become significantly important in a fuller appreciation of my journey to Orthodoxy. See Dr. Todd M. Johnson, "Christianity is Fragmented – Why?," *Gordon Conwell Theological Seminary*, https://www.gordonconwell.edu/blog/christianity-is-fragmented-why/, (November 6, 2019).

Chapter 9

"Zeal for Your house consumes me."
Psalm 69:9a

I have never been one who was satisfied to attend church on Sunday for the simple enjoyment of connecting with friends and to be inspired by an encouraging message. I have always been the girl that would annoy my pastors and Sunday school teachers, especially when I would be in a season of delving into Scripture. They could expect to be peppered with non-stop questions from a zealous teenager who eagerly sought to understand God's word and what He requires of us. They would get calls from me asking questions like:

"Why is there a herd of pigs when Jesus casts out demons since Jews weren't allowed to have pigs?"

"Why don't we keep the sabbath anymore even though we keep the other nine commandments?"

"Why don't women cover their heads in church?"

Often, I found the answers ranged from unsatisfying to downright bizarre. Take the last question for example, about 1 Corinthians 11:6-7, stating a woman is to cover her head during prayer: one response I would often receive was, "It was written to that time and culture and doesn't apply to us anymore." That just sparked more questions for me:

"How is it just a couple of lines before, the Bible tells us it is okay to eat or drink anything and that still counts, but then just a few sentences later, when it says women are to cover their heads, that part doesn't count anymore?[20] How does only part of a passage expire? And who decided that? And when?"

Now you see how I drove people crazy in my journey to understand my faith.

Another common interpretation of that passage was it is shameful for a woman to be bald, so the Bible is saying that women should not shave their heads. That one hurt my brain. I could not help but wonder if women shaving their head in that time was such a problem that they had to tell us in the Bible not to do it.

My barrage of questions would inevitably be met with a spiritual backhand where I would be admonished to let it go and was warned that I was being legalistic, like the Pharisees, which is offensive to Jesus.

I took this warning very seriously as offending Jesus was the last thing I wanted to do. The ramifications were terrifying and all too familiar from my childhood. Perhaps you can begin to see how my past abuse had primed me to fully embrace the concept of God the Father as wrathful and One who could strike out at any time. This image of the Father was not my perception solely because of my history. It was truly the teaching in that denomination. I once heard our youth pastor preach a sobering message warning that there *is* a point where we commit one sin too many, then God is done with us. And it does not have anything to do with how big the sin is, just when God hits his limit. His reference was a passage from Proverbs 1:24-26:

---

[20] Here I purposely used the verbiage of, "the Bible says," and not, "as Saint Paul wrote," as this was my Protestant thinking.

> "But since you refuse to listen when I call and no one pays attention when I stretch out my hand, since you disregard all My advice and do not accept My rebuke, I in turn will laugh when disaster strikes you; I will mock when calamity overtakes you."

I will never forget how he took time to unpack each part of that passage and emphasize that God the Father will laugh at us and mock us in our calamity because we brought it on ourselves. I was tormented because there was no way to know which sin will be the one too many.

How could I know that I was still on God's good side? How could I be sure I was not deceiving myself? What about the counterfeit Christianity my grandma warned me about, where you *feel* like everything is okay, but you are actually damned and will not find out until it is too late? What was it that the Lord wanted me to do, that if I do not do it, could land me in hell?

When I searched for relief from this torment, I asked for help from friends I respected. They would always assure me that I could be certain I was still saved because if I was not, my heart would have grown cold and hard. The torment itself was evidence that I had the right heart. Then they would tell me to let go of the torment and take comfort in the promise of my salvation that is in Jesus alone, in the payment He made on the cross to take away God's wrath.[21] Synopsized, what they were saying was, "Don't be tormented, even though we just told you it's your torment that's the proof that you're still okay."

---

[21] The theology of Jesus making a payment of His own life to God the Father to appease the wrath due to us is called Penal Substitutionary Atonement and is considered dogma in Protestant Christianity.

The next few decades would prove to be a brutal cycle of seasons of fervent study and trying to understand God and His word, followed by chastisement for being legalistic, leading to discouragement and spending weeks, sometimes months away from church, only to miss the Lord and start all over again.

The whole thing was an awful mess.

Chapter 10

*"I was glad when they said to me,
'Let us go into the house of the Lord.'"
Psalm 122:1*

Many years later, two children, a failed marriage, and countless cycles of pursuing God and giving up, I married the love of my life, Thilo Young. Handsome, principled, and above all, brilliant, he and I would have many conversations about God, theology, and the important matters of life. Come to find out, it wasn't only me who was not designed to sit through a Sunday service. I finally had a partner. Thilo and I would regularly find ourselves at a restaurant after service, engaged in animated dialogue about the teaching of that day. "Can you believe when pastor read about the father of the Prodigal son killing the fatted calf, and the Message Bible stated it as 'barbequed beef!?'" Together, he and I would laugh and cringe at some of the terrible theology we heard.

It was because of our passion that we would always end up in some sort of leadership role in the church—usually involving young people. I think for us, the younger generation always held a promise of hope. The youth were still fresh and not jaded in their faith. Besides that, our passion for theology and truth often left us outcasts within our own age group. We were not the favorites at Bible studies. We'd push back on the all too common Bible study method of "What does this passage mean to you?" We wanted to know what it meant to the writer and his audience! I think I felt the discomfort of being the "odd one" more than Thilo. It often happened that I would be excitedly sharing some historical background on a passage or the deeper meaning of a word translated in Scripture with one of the church ladies, only to be met with glazed over, painfully bored expressions. It just seemed we didn't fit with our own. However, on the other hand, the young people were eager to receive what we had to offer. They were excited to learn and their enthusiasm brought us great joy.

Thilo, had just concluded a season of teaching a robust study on how we got the Bible we have today—the canon. Even with as involved as he and I had been in our faith for so long, some of what he discovered in his research was quite surprising, even shocking from a Protestant standpoint, especially when considering the idea of the inerrancy of Scripture.

Another note here or the rest will not make sense: In the Protestant world, inerrancy of the Bible is critical. Every word, every fact, every single thing has to be 100% factual as it is the foundation of the Protestant faith. As a matter of fact, an explanation of the belief was most clearly stated to me by a reputable Protestant theologian. He said that after the last apostle died (and by the last apostle, referring to the 12, not the 70), oral tradition was no longer trustworthy. *Only* that which had been written down was valid. And that the Church itself was *founded* and built on the Bible.

Protestantism rejects oral tradition and is skeptical of anything written by anyone other than the Gospel writers and St. Paul. That means in order for Protestantism to stand, the Bible absolutely *has* to be perfect. For the Orthodox Christian, this is not so. We have the entire history of the Church to confirm that which is critical to our faith. For us, the truth that Jesus was crucified and raised from the dead goes far beyond the pages of the Bible. We have consistent teaching about Jesus that went out far and wide to all the countries surrounding Israel immediately after Pentecost. Therefore, we do not have to anxiously try to reconcile if the centurion met Jesus on the road himself or if he sent his servant. For us, if it was ever discovered there was an error in the document, it would by no means disqualify the validity of everything else in it. Now back to the story.

I recall our little rag-tag group sitting in the living room at a friend's house as Thilo began to unpack for us the formation of the canon. I clearly was not the only one squirming inside. As I looked around the room of typically enthusiastic learners ranging from 15 to 40 years old, their reactions were very much the same; raised eyebrows, shifting back and forth in their seats, looks of skepticism. Thilo was saying things like the Bible wasn't even assembled for over 300 years, and even then, deciding what was going to be included was not entirely cut and dry. Some books were highly contested yet made it in—barely. Others were *super* close but did not make the cut. And those extra books that clearly did not belong? Many of them were highly esteemed and quoted in the early Church. This new information was all very undoing.

I wouldn't say that as Evangelical Protestants we thought the Bible fell from the sky. In truth, we simply did not give much thought to it at all. If anyone would have ever asked me, I guess I would have said the disciples wrote the Bible as God dictated it to them and that's what all early Christians used when they would gather together in their house churches to pray. Easy-peasy. Oh, and all those "extra books" used by the Catholics, I along with all my other Protestant friends, would clearly agree those are *not* scripture and do *not* belong in the Bible.

Because of who God made my husband to be, for him this was not undoing, but captivating. It was a catalyst that would launch Thilo into an adventure to discover more. And he did not have to go far. Just down the street from my place of employment, there was a large church—"the Mosque," some of my friends called it in jest, because of its great dome and grandeur. In front of the building there was a sign that read, "Saint John Coptic Orthodox Church, See of Alexandria." Thilo knew that very little changes in the Orthodox tradition, so perhaps he could time-travel by attending one of their services.

I admit, I had no interest in joining him on his maiden voyage; off he went, just him and two dear friends of ours. I was quite accustomed to the duration of church services I had attended for over 40 years, hovering around about an hour to an hour and a half. I sat at home, bored and my stomach was grumbling. When I looked at the clock, it had already been two hours and not a word! What could he possibly be doing for this long?! Between my boredom and my empty stomach, my patience had reached its limit. I texted him to ask how soon he would be coming home. I could have never imagined I would get the response I received from him; "Service is still going." I was shocked. Two hours and *still* going? I guess you could say this was my first of what eventually would be many long services with *no* breakfast.

The entire following week, my husband who was often known for being gruff, grumpy, and not easily amused, was an entirely different person. He was smiling and gentle. For the first time in a very long time, he seemed to have peace. (I believe this event foreshadowed the baptismal name he would come to take, Irenaeus, meaning peace).

It was sometime during this week that Thilo had invited me to lunch to meet the young priest he had encountered during his visit. We were first to arrive at Red Robin, a nearby burger restaurant. Thilo positioned himself in the waiting area, facing the door, watching for his new friend. He was giddy. Yes. Giddy. Again, Mr. gruff and grumpy was acting like a schoolboy with a new super-best friend. I wondered to myself, "Who is this guy we're meeting???" In walked a young priest in a black cassock. Thilo jumped up to greet him but I wasn't sure how I felt. He looked like a combination of a catholic priest and a Muslim. And this is how I was introduced to Abouna Daniel Habib.

Thilo and Abouna Daniel did most of the talking through lunch. I don't recall saying much as I wasn't really interested in this exploration of Orthodox Christianity as much as I was interested in defending against it. As a matter of fact, it was at that lunch we made it clear to Abouna that we had no intention of converting. We were just looking to learn. He warned us that many Protestants come just to learn but end up converting. I laughed inside of myself. "Yeah. No worries. Not a chance of that happening here."

Thilo was still walking on air. In utter disbelief of what kind of miracle could have transpired that could change the man who had lovingly earned the nickname "Grinch" among the young people we taught, I absolutely had to see what this was all about.

The following Sunday, I tagged along. Walking in, the sanctuary was certainly not anything like the churches I attended. First off, it was huge. I had been in large churches before. In the Protestant world, they are called mega-churches and can be larger than a shopping mall. True story. It wasn't just the size of the church, that was a bit overwhelming.

As I looked around, it was far from the décor I was familiar with. Rather than the cool hues of trendy modern colors and an attractively designed stage to feature the band and singers, I was surrounded by a sea of red carpet and way more gold and pictures of saints than was to my liking. Instead of comfortable and attractive individual seats for churchgoers, before me was sanctuary filled with long, very *un*-comfortable, wooden pews.

An older Egyptian woman stood at the back of the church, facing one of the icons. She lit a candle, said a prayer, touched the picture and kissed her hand. Then she crossed herself and made her way to her seat. Now I was *very* uneasy.

Enter a rather harried, serious-looking, middle-aged, bearded man, obviously a priest, head-down, trying to quickly make his way to the front of the church. He was donned in a rather severe looking black robe, a giant cross hanging mid-torso, and Crocs. It was Abouna Daniel! There were few people in the pews at this point, but still the scene was somewhat humorous. Despite his obvious focus and determination to quickly make his way to the front of the church, he was intercepted here and there as a person would jump up to kiss his hand. This was an odd place to say the least. Between people kissing the priest's hand and a woman praying to saints, I was definitely feeling all of this was incredibly *not* okay.

If it was not for Thilo's sake, I would have left at that moment—and the service had not even begun. Even so, I was certain I would *not* be back. Ever. In the front of the church there was a huge arched opening covered by a heavy red velvet curtain. Suddenly Abouna appeared, drawing back the curtain, maintaining the same forward-moving focused pace he had when he entered the church. He was chanting something in another language. It was almost like we had caught him in the middle of a stream of thought, making no eye-contact with the congregation. The small handful of people peppered throughout the large room sprung to their feet as if they were invisibly called to attention. I awkwardly followed suit. The first question that came to mind was, "Where is everyone?" Was service really starting with fifteen people in this gigantic church? Then, as I looked around the room, here came my next awkward realization: all the women were sitting on the *other* side—and wearing scarves on their heads.

Suddenly my ears were blessed to hear a little bit of English! The congregation joined the priest as he began, "Our Father who art in heaven. . ." Yes! I remembered this one from my childhood! I eagerly began to join in, but then, unexpectedly the initial proclamation dissolved into a mumble then silence. I looked around trying to figure out what just happened. The people looked like odd statues with their heads bowed in silence and their hands raised, palms up. Then the silence was broken when Abouna loudly proclaimed, "Let us give thanks. . ." Again, the initially audible words from the congregation melted away into a mumble then nothing, leaving me standing there in silence trying to figure out what was happening. I felt like I just accidently stumbled onto the stage during the ballet performance of *Swan Lake*, and everyone else knew the choreography. I just wanted to find the exit.

My stomach was in a knot. I hated this. And all I could think was "How long is this going to be?" It was right about that moment, at the height of my discomfort, a young woman came and quietly introduced herself to us. She said her name was Mariam and that Abouna Daniel had let her know that we were new and might need some help through the liturgy. At last! Someone to rescue me! I was eternally grateful to not be left alone to embarrass myself in this conglomeration of stand up, sit down, stand back up again, now cross yourself—it was too much.

Mariam started at the beginning, and as they say in *The Sound of Music*, that is, "a very good place to start." She gestured to the red carpet that spread through the enormous sanctuary. She leaned in and whispered, "In all our churches, our carpet is red because it represents the blood of Christ and the blood of the martyrs which is the foundation of the Church." I was literally stunned. In the churches I had attended, the color of the carpet was a much more aesthetically pleasing contemporary color—at the same time—I was also familiar with the behind-the-scenes fights that would occur over who would get to choose something that complimented the color palette of the rest of the interior design. And as far as symbolism? Mostly, it represented who had the final word in decorating.

Next, Mariam pointed to the four pillars and said that they represent the four gospel writers. She went on to explain the censer as Saint Mary, as it holds a burning coal, yet is not consumed, Saint Mary carried God in her womb and was not consumed. The entire service she enlightened us about icons, the priests robes, how the Coptic Church was founded by Saint Mark....*Saint Mark*! Keep in mind that in the church world I came from, if your church was founded before 1975, that was impressive. This place was *rich* with depth, history, and meaning. Everything was intentional.

When I left that day, I was greatly confused as to how I felt about what I had just experienced. There was much I did not like: the different languages, the feeling like an outsider because I did not know the "choreography," and definitely, I did not care for all the icons and people praying to saints. Still there were a couple of things that I would never forget; One was the meaningfulness of everything. Every color, every piece used in the altar, every gesture of the hand in the icons, everything was telling the story of the Lord. I recognized that, despite my inability to understand, their voices were still going out. Another thing was the Gospel reading that Sunday was of the Samaritan woman, whom I later came to know as Saint Photini. She had always been dear to my heart. A courageous woman, though rough around the edges and even at that moment, not living as she should. When her sin was exposed by this Stranger, her desire for the Lord was so strong, it did not shake her a bit. Rather than, "What business is it of yours if I'm married or not?!" she responds to the Lord asking Him where the correct place to worship is. I related to her so much, and here on my first orthodox Sunday, her story was read and commemorated. Ironically, the week before, with Thilo's maiden voyage, the Gospel reading was the Prodigal Son. How I love our Lord's sense of humor!

After the service, there was an unexplainable peace that lingered the rest of the day, if not longer. It was mysterious. It was tangible. And yet at the same time, not. It was much like the lingering aroma of incense or the melody of the hymns echoing in my mind. It was a strange feeling.

This place was different. It did not feel like *a* church. It felt like...*the* Church.

Chapter 11

"What is truth?"
John 18:38

Through what felt like no choice of our own, we were swept into an adventure that was underway. While Thilo and I had absolutely no intention of leaving our Protestant home church, let alone converting to this ancient form of Christianity, we both felt that at the very least we could collect some of its beautiful historical truths and take them back to share with our friends in our own congregation.

Thilo took the lead on researching then sharing his discoveries with me. He mentioned many times that it was Saint Irenaeus' statement that if you want to know what was taught by the apostles, look at the churches they established and see where they agree. When Thilo heard that, it was challenge accepted. One of the first gems he discovered was the *Didache*, a very early church document dating back to the early to mid-nineties AD. I had no idea that topics such as baptism, communion, and salvation were already discussed at such an early date.

I am mentioning Thilo a lot. That is because it was Thilo that was immersing himself into this research. In the years I had known him, it was common for some topic to grab his interest and he would run with it for months, even years. For a time, it was studying the Biblical teaching of the age of the Earth. Later it was debating atheists in an online platform. Even the very thing that started this whole adventure, was his studying of how we got the Bible we have today. To me, Thilo studying about ancient Christianity was just the next thing in his long line of projects.

I typically enjoyed when he would share with me what he discovered. It was fascinating to learn what these esteemed writers were saying during the birth of Christianity. However again, stepping so far back into the past of the history of Christianity was coming with a mixture of emotions. It was certainly intriguing but what he was discovering throughout a myriad of writings, turned everything we had ever known or believed about salvation, baptism, and communion on its head. I suppose this was the second upheaval of what I thought I knew about my own faith and it was once again, very undoing.

It was becoming clear that this adventure into exploring Orthodoxy was not Thilo's typical temporary fascination in learning something new. This was beginning to divide us.

Chapter 12

"Do not think that I came to bring peace to the Earth. I did not come to bring peace, but a sword."
Matthew 10:34b

As Thilo learned more and more, his passion grew. As his passion grew, so did my concern. It was evident where this was heading. Trying to be a good wife, I attempted to be supportive. My support wasn't fake. I was genuinely interested in the history, but I had no interest in leaving my longtime church family. And honestly, as we began spending more time in Coptic liturgies and less time in what was familiar to me, I felt like I was dying inside.

My whole life, the place where I would go to meet the Lord was in what we called in the Protestant church, "worship," It was powerful, moving music, intimate lyrics, and vocalists on the stage leading the singing, faces wrought with emotion. Here, I felt like I had stepped into heaven. With my hands stretched to the sky, I would pour my heart out to the Lord in song. But as we attended more liturgies, the odd tunes of the Coptic chants, with clanging symbols was not feeding my soul as I had been fed before.

This was when the next real, wave of fear, hit me. Thilo was headed towards Orthodoxy. Until now, I just followed behind him. But how far was I going to go? Would I be willing to accept and be baptized into a form of Christianity that I had theological problems with? Where they pray to saints, venerate St. Mary, confess to priests—all the things I had been taught against, and had in turn taught against for decades? Also, what if we became part of this foreign church and something happened to him? He would be gone and I would be stuck in his church of *his* faith—not my own. The answer was no. Simply no. I loved my husband, but one of the things that brought us together is that we are both principled. There was no way I would make such a compromise. Either this would have to truly become my faith, or we would have to live separate spiritual lives, which the thought of also killed me inside.

I shared with Abouna Daniel how I felt like I was dying inside. He suggested that, since liturgies are so long, perhaps I could continue to attend a local Protestant service, then head over afterwards to the remainder of the Coptic Orthodox service. He wisely made me agree to a timeframe of a few months, just to give Coptic Orthodoxy a fair chance. I am a reasonable woman and that was a reasonable request. I agreed.

During this time Abouna also gave me an *Agpeya* (Book of Hours) and simple prayer rule. For readers who are unfamiliar with a prayer rule, it is a sort of prescription given by your spiritual father. It is important that he be the one to prescribe it as he guides with wisdom. If left to our own devices, we can lean towards laziness or pride—doing too much or too little.

Through my prayer rule, and through Abouna Daniel's wise decision to not ask me to cut off the Protestant form of worship that was so important to me, I made an unexpected discovery. Remember how I said I felt like I was dying inside because my soul was not being fed as it had been fed before? I discovered in the daily prayer, thanksgiving, repentance, Gospel reading…my soul was indeed being fed. It was being fed *all week*, not once a week. And Sunday was changing for me. It was no longer a time to be fed. It was not a time to *take*, it was a time to *give*! It was a time to bring offerings to the Lord; praise, thanksgiving, repentance, and petitions! We bring all that we have collected during the week, good and bad, and we bring it to Him.

Until now, the church "service" meant to serve the people. Everything was directed to the people. The rehearsals for worship so that the performance would be spot-on for the congregation. The engaging message delivered in a dynamic way. The use of media and video to be engaging... and all was measured by an imaginary score card of how *I* felt when I left church. Here, in Orthodox Christianity, liturgy is "the work of the people." It is rightly the Lord to whom we offer our service. It is all about Him. And even with that, His generosity cannot be restrained. When we make it *all* about Him, we offer prayer, praise, bread, and wine and what does He give us in return? His very own body and blood and the remission of our sins. Every week is like being baptized anew.

I cannot begin to express the monumental shift in my thinking, in how I viewed everything. Suddenly, the singing that I felt was my only connection to Life Himself, looked juvenile and self-serving. What was happening to me? How was it that everything I thought I knew, backward and forward, was now becoming empty and irrational?

In his own way, Thilo was experiencing the same thing. How could we not ask ourselves; If we could be so entirely wrong about such important matters, what else might we be unaware of?

Ironically, it was not Orthodox Christianity that was demanding me to abandon Protestantism. It was events that happened in our visits to our Protestant church home that were pushing me in the direction of Orthodox Christianity. Two such events still stand out clearly in my mind.

Once, during communion, (which my husband and I opted not to participate in. We had come to believe what the Church has said, as long ago as the Didache written around 70 AD. Communion, that true communion is the actual body and blood of Christ, with strict adherences as to its distribution), the pastor stood up and took the tiny piece of unleavened bread and the little cup of grape juice, and holding them up he authoritatively spoke to the audience, "This is just bread. And this is just juice. There is nothing magical about it. But it reminds us of what Jesus did on the cross for us, so we should remember the sacrifice He made on our behalf." I was cringing inside. No power. No remission of sins. Not the Body and Blood of Christ. It wasn't simply that this denomination, like many, did not *believe* in the historical teaching of the Eucharist. The pastor was systematically and openly rejecting the teachings to the congregation. I felt like yelling, "Work with me here! I'm trying to find a reason to stay with you, but you're drawing a line in the sand!"

The other event was my teenage niece's baptism. Again, the pastor declared, "There is nothing magical about this water. It does not do anything. It does not save her. It is just an outward profession of an inward decision that she already made and now she wants the world to know." Again, openly, shamelessly rejecting the ancient Christian teachings of baptism.[22]

I was dumbfounded. Why? Why does it even have to be said what baptism or communion does not do? Why not just stick to what it is you are doing and the reason? Forty years as a Protestant, I never saw myself as Protestant, only Christian. But now I was seeing it everywhere. We were still *protesting*.

---

[22] The pastor's words were a rejection of Jesus' own words in John 3:5.

Chapter 13

"'Do You not care that we are perishing?'"
Mark 4:38

While we may have started this adventure with sunny skies and smooth sailing, the skies were growing dark and the water was troubling. Much of what we were learning was as we expected; it was beautiful, meaningful, and enriching. But there were too many beliefs, important beliefs, that we were discovering that were *the exact opposite* in Orthodox Christianity than what we came to hold true as Protestants.

One such foundational doctrine, was how one is "saved," or even what saved means. In our non-denominational/Evangelical Protestant teachings, it was emphasized, beyond all measure, that we contribute *nothing* towards our salvation. "Salvation" or "saved" in Protestant understanding, means to be rescued from the just punishment of hell. As I mentioned before, a single, honest heartfelt prayer in which you accept the payment of suffering and death that Jesus made to the Father on your behalf, and you were in *for good*. However, the teachings we were discovering from very early Christianity, and broadly believed, were all in agreement and clearly and emphatically painted salvation as something much different than crime and punishment. (Remember Saint Irenaeus' test: early, universal, and sustained teachings.) In ancient Christianity (Orthodoxy), salvation is something that we co-operate with the Lord in, though not in a fifty-fifty kind of way. And salvation means so much more than having your legal debt of sins paid for so you do not have to go to hell. In the Ancient Church, sin was and has always been, seen as at times, a transgression we are accountable for but also it is a condition, a sickness—something to be healed from. There is no moment where everything is suddenly made right. It is a long arduous process that is dependent on the Great Physician's skill and love, and our collaboration with Him, availing ourselves of the medicines of the soul: baptism, chrismation, confession, fasting, prayer, almsgiving, and above all, the Holy Eucharist.

And there it is again—the Holy Eucharist. Is it merely juice and bread to reflect upon the punishment Jesus took for us? Or is it truly the life-giving flesh that He took from the Lady of us all, the Holy Theotokos, Saint Mary, making it one with His divinity, without mingling, without confusion, and without alteration?

Please, hear my words about the focus of Protestant communion: to remember the punishment Jesus took for us. Their teaching focuses nearly entirely on the cross, where Jesus stepped in to take the chastisement from the Father who poured out His wrath on the Son, with lashes, humiliation, and a crown of thorns—*even turning away from the Son*—because a just God requires that *someone* had to pay for all our crimes (sins) against God.

Forgive me as I take a moment to interrupt my own train of thought to emphasize how critical understanding the above mindset is. There is a Greek word I have recently learned; *phronema*. It is often translated as "mind' in the Scriptures, but a better translation might be "mindset." The teaching that our sins are a crime that a just Judge absolutely *must* require punishment to be paid in order to release the sinner from their debt is the *phronema*, the mindset of the Protestant church. It, like leaven or yeast, leavens the whole lump. Everything is viewed through that lens.

Even having been in the Church for more than 10 years now, I still struggle with putting on the mind of Christ and putting away this old way of thinking. A recent example was a shift from understanding who I am in the eyes of God. To Him, I am beloved. Yet the rancid stench of my old mindset still lingers where I am defined as a sinner saved by grace.

The first definition is who God created me to be and who I am underneath the soiling of sin. The other is a wrong identity, one that defines me by what I do. How can I begin to tell you the tears that flowed to know how the Lover of my soul sees me? That He does not define me as a wretch who by His mercy—the kind of mercy that determines if I stomp on a bug or not—merely *allows* me to enter into Heaven because it is legally just because the price has been paid?

Back to the storyline: Thilo and I read the writings of the fathers of the early Church, again, who unanimously spoke of something much bigger, much more significant, not solely focused on the cross—the Incarnation—God humbling Himself and becoming man. It was Jesus' life of humility, love, restoring the relationship between mankind and God, as well as between human and human, and the relationship between all humanity and creation. It was His death, where He entered into death as fully man, and overcame it as fully God. It was His resurrection, triumphant in the defeat of death and raising us with Him. It was even the sending of His Holy Spirit to fill us and teach us. And at no time, was there division of the Holy Trinity. The Father, Son, and Spirit have always been working together towards our healing since the fall of Adam and Eve. "[He has] not abandoned us to the end."

As we discovered each of these teachings mentioned, and many more besides, my husband and I were slowly being forced into a place of realization that Orthodox Christianity was either really, really right or really, really wrong. Either we had just encountered the true faith—ancient Christianity—or we were being led away from the true faith—Protestant Christianity—and we were about become cut off from God.

There were no more delightful moments of enrichment and fascination in learning something new. We were now in the middle of a sea, thick darkness above us, the waters now fully churning beneath us, and we could no longer see the shore.

We were truly terrified.

Chapter 14

"'You are out of your mind! Too much learning is driving you insane!'"
Acts 26:24

Up until now, I have, somewhat intentionally, neglected to share the part of my journey that involves my place of employment. During this season, I worked for a Protestant apologetics ministry. (Apologetics is simply a fancy term for defense, and this particular ministry focuses on offering a defense for faith that is grounded in science and reason.) Before I lead into this part of the story I feel I must let you know I'll be sharing some painful struggles I encountered at my job along the way. I have decided to tell this part as it was specifically these struggles that launched me farther into the Orthodox faith. Also, because some of the accounts are not the most flattering, I am also compelled to say of this organization that it was, and continues to be, a wonderful, integrous place with truly amazing people.

With that foundation laid, it will be helpful to know that in the Protestant world, to explore different expressions of Christianity is encouraged and celebrated. Most of my friends thought it was cool that my husband and I were spending so much time learning about ancient Christianity. I often heard, "I'm so glad you're enjoying it! Whatever works for you!" The problem was they did not know that by this point, I was *not* enjoying it. Each new thing I learned slowly drove a wedge between my contemporary understanding of the Christian faith and the ancient; it threatened to split my entire world apart. And while the idea of "whatever works for you" may be common in the broader Protestant community, not everyone feels that way—especially in an organization whose whole existence is to defend accurate (Protestant) beliefs.

In my workplace, my exploration of Orthodoxy seemed to be hardly noticed. But when I would share something new I had learned, it most often would be received with a semi-interested nod or a slight correction. In an environment that is highly academic, learning is encouraged. I am sure there was little concern that my exploration would develop into anything significant other than perhaps a greater understanding of Church history. However, once it became evident to a few coworkers that I appeared to be moving towards converting, things changed. They saw me moving towards a belief that they understood to include all the *perceived* ills (emphasis is mine) of the Roman Catholic church such as the worship of Saint Mary, bizarre beliefs like eating Jesus' flesh and drinking His blood. But perhaps the most heinous was the belief that humanity is saved by works, not solely by Christ's finished work on the cross.

It was this growing concern that was the catalyst to my first unexpected experience at work. It was with a man who I had known for six years and was renowned for his gentleness. I very much considered him a dear friend and still do. I made a comment—what it was, I cannot even recall now—and with a raised voice, he responded angrily, "Christianity is not a monolith!" I was so taken aback at the passion of this otherwise quiet man, I did not even dare to ask what he meant by that. I just quickly dropped the topic at hand. I was stunned. I had never seen him angry before nor since so his reaction shook me, you could even say wounded me deeply. I hoped this to be an anomaly, but it was only beginning.

Not long after, another coworker who I also consider a dear friend, a very studious and intelligent man, came to me with a stack of photocopies in hand. He had a serious expression and spoke to me in a sober tone, "You *do* realize that you're becoming a heretic, right?" The stack of paper was myriads of citations warning that the Copts are false Christians who not only hold all the troubling beliefs held by the Catholics, but also deny Christ's human and divine natures.

Again, I did not anticipate any of this, but nevertheless, here I was in the middle of it. Part of me wanted to defend Coptic Orthodoxy and explain the inaccuracy of these allegations, especially the misunderstanding of calling Copts Monophysites but who was I kidding? I was terribly ill-equipped and would be in way over my head arguing with someone of his apologetics caliber. This was another deep wound, not just because what was said, but who it came from. Truly, I was becoming afraid. Would this cause me to lose my friends? And I hadn't even considered, would it cause me to lose my job? I believe that God in His goodness made me aware that this friend had not ceased to care about me. On the contrary, his sternness stemmed from a deep care for my eternal soul. Though it stung, that truth brought me a bitter-sweet comfort.

Meanwhile, there also was unseen movement happening below the surface of the day-to-day workings in the organization. A few members of the leadership were beginning to meet to address the growing problem of "bad theology" potentially seeping into the ministry through me.

How I learned of these conversations was yet another painful wound. One afternoon, the entire staff was asked to gather in the conference room to discuss the newly revised statement of faith. (A statement of faith is a carefully worded formal declaration that lays out specific religious beliefs the organization adheres to. To be a part of that organization, one must affirm that they uphold these beliefs. A statement of faith is very common in religious organizations).

We listened to the leadership roll out the list of changes that had been implemented.

First: Signing the statement of faith would not only be mandatory upon time of hire, but would also need to be signed and resubmitted each year of employment.

Next: New language was introduced that was much tighter and exclusive than before. The previous language encompassed most forms of Christianity. However, the new wording was admittedly designed to be distinctly Protestant and would not easily allow any practicing Catholic or Orthodox to be employed by the ministry.

One example of the "tighter language" was the now more emphatic assertion that the Bible is inerrant and the final authority on all matters to which it speaks.

I remind you as to why inerrancy is so important to Protestants. In one fell swoop, it once again proclaims its rejection from the traditions of the Roman Catholic Church, which it divorced itself from more than 500 years ago, while it also declares that Scripture alone (*Sola scriptura*) is the foundation of all truth. And without tradition, the written word has to be 100% perfect, without error. A personal observation is that this divorce from the traditions and teachings of the Church has not freed us from human interpretation but rather left every person to fend for themselves and to do their best to interpret, either by trying to follow the feelings of their heart as a leading of the Holy Spirit, or immersion in language and history, or both.

The result is being cut off from 2,000 years of a wealth of wisdom has led to innumerable new and different understandings.

Back to the story: it was in this moment as I sat in the meeting, my brain screamed, *"Whose interpretation of the Bible?!"*

One co-worker who was also a friend raised her hand. Though she was addressing the leadership, her eyes glanced in my direction as she asked, "What if someone doesn't *entirely* agree with the wording?" It was obvious this question was in my defense. The reply was, "You don't have to sign it. But you don't have to work here either." That was a gut punch if there ever was one.

I raised my hand to inquire if the leadership realized that the new restrictive language would disallow the ministry from hiring valuable people from the Catholic and Orthodox communities. It was stated in front of all, "We knew you would have a problem with that. Yes. We purposely rewrote the statement of faith to be distinctly Protestant, not just Christian."

I was hit especially hard by the words,

"We *knew* you'd have a problem with that...."

"We"?

There was a discussion, and my name was brought up as a part of that discussion? I could feel an awkward discomfort from some of the people in the room who were in the know about my upcoming baptism into Orthodoxy. And I perceived a sort of victory from others. I was embarrassed and hurt.

No more wondering if I was being paranoid thinking this was because of me. It *was* because of me and now it was out in the open. The entire staff was expected to sign and return the document by the end of the week. This was by no means at the level of confessing before the governor like we frequently read in the synaxarium, but it certainly felt like it in some way. Suddenly there was a clock ticking and a decision to be made. What side would I stand on? All of this was already coming at me and I had not even been baptized yet!

Can I just say, thank God for our Abounas? In my old life, a huge decision like this would fall on my shoulders alone. I would be left to pray and use the previously mentioned prayer and best guess as to which feelings were my own and which were direction from the Holy Spirit. But now I was entering the Church and had a spiritual father, glory to God. My Abouna showed me there was a way to remain integrous and sign the statement in good conscience. (That discussion remains between me and him). The Lord was gentle with His daughter. No martyrdom would be asked of me today. As required, I signed and turned in the new distinctly Protestant statement of faith.

Very glad to have all that behind me, I carried on business as usual. Unexpectedly, a day or two after the statements were due to be turned in, a coworker came by my desk and curiously inquired, "So? Did you sign the statement?" When I looked up at him, he seemed to have a "gotcha" expression on his face. I responded, "yes." He was visibly surprised, or better said, shocked. His reaction ignited irritation in me and a question of my own, "Are you asking everyone this?" He quickly realized he was wading into potentially legal murky waters so, without responding, he made a hasty exit.

Now I was angry. After decades of hearing from Protestant believers that anyone who confesses that Jesus is Christ is the Son of God, and that He died for our sins and rose from the dead, is a Christian. Now I had been yelled at, warned I was becoming a heretic, and embarrassed in front of the entire staff. An entire company policy was changed or clarified because of me.

As the indignation began to grow in me, I argued in my own mind, "If Orthodox Christianity is just another expression of Christianity, then why the hostility and the threat of losing my friends and my job?"

The gauntlet had been thrown and the challenge was accepted.

I will conclude this chapter as I began it, stating my admiration for the ministry and the people I worked with. It was necessary to allow you to experience the pain and the passion as I did, as this moment was a critical fork in my road. With thanksgiving to God, I can say that those mentioned above, along with myself, have grown in grace and understanding in the decade that has followed.

Chapter 15

"'If anyone comes to me and does not hate father and mother...such a person cannot be My disciple.'"
Luke 14:26

What began as an innocent inquiry to learn more about my own faith, turned into a war. I felt like many people in my Protestant world had stated implicitly or explicitly, "It's us or them. Choose." Feeling strong, almost militant, I pictured 2,000 years of Orthodox Christians behind me and defiantly said, "I choose them." It is not the way I would have had it. I wanted to share with everyone the things we had learned and for others to know the truth. But it was *they* who rejected me—so be it. One Coptic person told me, "*Now you're protesting the right thing.*"

I had been telling my parents about my journey all along the way. They were not thrilled with everything I shared, especially when I invited them to our quickly approaching baptism. My mother skeptically challenged, "Why do you need to be baptized again?" I felt this an odd question coming from someone who had witnessed *many* individuals baptized two, three, four times. Re-baptized each time they had re-dedicated their life after having drifted away from the Lord for a time. But this was different. In her eyes, this Orthodox (and really in their mind "Roman Catholic") religion *was demanding* that I be re-baptized.

"Nobody has the right to tell you what to do when it comes to your relationship with God. *Nobody,*" was her response.

I tried to explain the finer points of apostolic succession, chrism, and so on. I might as well have been speaking Arabic with the little success I had explaining nuances of ancient Christianity, baptism, and even why I *wanted* to be re-baptized. Moreover, I was not only failing to communicate, but the harder I tried to explain, the more I offended my parents.

It hurt them to see what they perceived as me walking away from the grace of Christ to legalism. They made it clear they would not attend the baptism.

Chapter 16

"Suddenly the boat reached the shore where they were headed."
John 6:21b

The combination of those present—and absent—for our baptism on April 14, 2012, brought a bittersweetness. Many dear Protestant friends along with a gathering of new Coptic friends came to support us with their love and presence.

I faced West and declared to Satan and all his demons, "I renounce you, I renounce you, I renounce you," and turned to the East and declared with determination to my Lord, "I believe, I believe, I believe."

I believe *in one God—the Pantocrator.* ***I believe*** *in His only begotten Son.* ***I believe*** *in the Holy Spirit, and in one holy, catholic, and apostolic Church...*

Yes. I believe.

I was baptized "Anastasia." Resurrection. *I believe.*

Axia! Axia! Axia!

Easter liturgy seemed to take forever as I anxiously waited to receive Christ's Holy Body and precious true Blood for the first time, but then the time came. I was *incredibly* nervous. I never even witnessed someone taking communion as it was in an area not visible from the congregation, beside the altar. I calmed myself by thinking, "I'll just do whatever the people in front of me do." Oh, Egyptian hospitality. The women joyfully waved me, the newly baptized Coptic Christian, to the front of the line.

I tried to politely decline and fall behind them. That does not work in the Egyptian community. Terrified I approached Abouna, praying the Body would not fall out of my mouth, or that I would not swallow wrong and spill or choke on the Blood. It is humorous all the scenarios the imagination can come up with as to what could go wrong. That is except when a healthy dose of sobriety would be merited—like when a priest sits across from you at a restaurant and warns you that you are on a well-worn path to conversion.

Thank God, all went well.

I was exhausted, happy, and peaceful.

There is one more tradition I neglected to mention. About midway through Easter service, my husband and I were called to join the procession at the front of the church, and we each were handed a candle. As we walked, I took in the sea of smiles, the joyful chant of the long line of deacons that wrapped around a good portion of the large church, the bright sound of their symbols, the beautiful smell of incense in the air. I witnessed Psalm 68:18 embodied, "You ascended on high, leading a host of captives in Your train…" Absolutely saturated in God's love, I looked at my husband, Irenaeus—Peace—and knew the old had passed away. Everything was made new.

Anastasis—Resurrection.

Chapter 17

"Zeal for Your house..."
Psalm 69:9
(Orthodox Style)

Remember when I said that neither Thilo nor I were designed to simply sit in Sunday services? Converting to Coptic Orthodoxy hadn't changed that. Full of zeal, in less than a year, I found myself helping teach the youth. Within a year after that, it seemed that servants and priests were coming out of the woodworks asking us to share our conversion story. At first, out of habit I referred to our story as our testimony, as it was called in our old world, but we had left that behind, so the title of our talk was aptly changed to "Our Journey to Orthodoxy."

We were invited to speak after liturgies, in adult meetings, youth meetings, even at a number of youth camps. It was amazing (and often humorous) to witness the impact of the story of our discovery of this beautiful faith. At times it was obvious the young people were envious of the passion we had for Orthodox Christianity. A passion that was unfamiliar to many of them, despite having been born into it. Other times, I could not help but be amused by the sheer incredulity and confusion on their faces when they would ask *why* we would leave the lights, the bands, the exciting sermons, and most importantly, the short services for long liturgies and lots of fasting. They could not figure us out!

Though I had a great zeal for my newfound faith and loved sharing the journey, there was a growing gnawing in my conscience. This felt too much like the old paradigm that I had left—where a person with a great story and a dynamic presentation becomes a sort of celebrity. Everything I had learned from the fathers during my catechesis, encouraged humility, smallness, and, in the words of St. Ephraim, "Slowly, slowly."

I felt I knew nothing at all about my faith and I was supposed to teach others, especially youth, about Orthodoxy? Two such occasions still vividly stand out in my mind.

Once I was asked to give a teaching on "The fullness of time." I had no idea what that was or what it meant. Of course, I did my usual protesting, but obediently crammed as if for a test, and by God's grace, muddled through.

The second, and this one still haunts me to this day, was a request to teach at a weekend youth conference. Thilo and I were to address how to worship in spirit and in truth. I have to admit, I was literally sick to my stomach when we were invited. Again, I knew nothing about this. Worse off, the information I did have was from a very skewed form of Protestant Christianity. I knew what worshipping in spirit and truth *was not*, but I had no idea in the Orthodox faith, what it *was*. I felt, and please note that this was just a feeling, that my desire to not teach, was received as false humility and was viewed as something I needed to overcome.

Now, years later, I know I was right. I knew nothing of worshipping in spirit and in truth. I personally have only recently begun to break the surface of unfathomable depths of prayer and worship, and yet, we "taught" these young people.

Our calls to teach were not without a safety net. Abounas were always nearby and assured us that if we strayed, they would correct. We were also urged over and over of the need of our perspective, from "outsiders," to spur to jealousy, if possible, a zeal in cradle Copts for their own faith.

We said yes to every invitation in obedience to our Mother the Church. As we visited more and more parishes, we unexpectedly began witnessing something we never anticipated: Protestant practices in *our* beautiful Orthodox Church.

One such evening still stands out to me. We were invited to speak at a particular youth meeting. We met the youth "leader," the word usage of which made the hair on my neck bristle.[23] He was a young, charismatic guy, with frosted blonde tips on his hair. Super-cool and relatable. I narrowed my eyes and looked at him with skepticism. I was not impressed. We made our way to a rooftop where the youth were gathered on a warm summer night. We had arrived in time for the praying of the *Agpeya*, which, much to our surprise (or should I say horror) was followed by Protestant worship songs led with an acoustic guitar. What was *this*?? This was the bad theology, the showmanship, and emotional manipulation we had left behind. Not just left behind, but that our renouncement had cost us so dearly—now *in* The Church?!

Should you find yourself arguing with me at this point and defending Protestant songs, I encourage you two-fold: Remember that I am telling you this story in the way I experienced it, with the zeal and fire of a new convert. Next, I *came* from the Protestant church, so I know a thing or two that extends beyond the beautiful music and lyrics (yes, I admitted beautiful). There is also often bad theology in the words and

---

[23] In our tradition, overseers are referred to as servants not leaders and for good reason. Servant denotes the proper humility one should have in ministry.

intentional way the music is written. When you hear these, pay attention how nearly all the words are about the love of Jesus—rarely anything about the Father or Holy Spirit. Often, there are beliefs that the Church rejected for 2,000 years, subtly imbedded in the song. An example is found in the beautiful melody, "How Deep the Father's Love for Us:"

> "How great the pain of searing loss,
> The Father turns His face away,
> As wounds which mar the Chosen One,
> Bring many sons to glory."

The Church, and I mean the *entire* holy, catholic, and apostolic Church, would *never* say that there was a division between the Father and the Son…ever.

Add to that, the music is written to usher the person into a place of worship. Re-translated, honestly, it is mood-music. Mood music is not evil, but it is *not* how Orthodox Christianity approaches worship for *so* many incredibly important reasons. I would also like to remind you how I shared with you earlier that this kind of "worship" was once the most important part of my life, but then I discovered how backwards, empty, self-serving, and wrong it is to bring this into a service that is supposed to be focused on giving an offering to God. My Orthodox brothers and sisters, how I wish I could help you to see the difference between worship and inspiration! And that if you were more knowledgeable about your faith, these inspirational songs might not be a threat to you, but until you do, they are.

Now, back to the story: as I watched what looked nearly exactly like youth meetings from the place that we had just left, my jaw clenched. This was not going to happen in the Orthodox Church. Not on our watch.

As we witnessed this Protestant infiltration from parish to parish, Thilo and I were on a crusade to "convert Copts to their own faith," as he would often say.

All roads, no matter the topic we were speaking on, lead to a comparison to heterodox (a scholastic way of saying bad) Protestant theology—and of course it would! It is what we knew and it is what we were passionate about.

Did you know that "passion" comes from the Latin *passio* or *pati* and means "suffer"? That is why in Orthodox Christianity, we call vices, passions. They bring us suffering. So when I say that Thilo and I were passionate against Protestant theology, it doesn't mean we were excited to teach about the differences. It means we were suffering. I will speak for myself. *I* was suffering. Once again, I was angry. In coming into Orthodox Christianity, each new thing I discovered about our faith, about confession, baptism, the Holy Body and Blood of Christ, *ev-er-y-thing* was the opposite. I felt as though I had been lied to my entire life leading up to Orthodoxy. Like when Jesus admonishes the Pharisees, saying, "You shut up the Kingdom of Heaven against men; for you neither go in yourselves, nor do you allow those who are entering to go in" (Matthew 23:23).

Have you ever noticed that often when people are suffering, they cause others to suffer? It can be intentional like when we're afraid for them and we want them to understand the danger they're in. Or unintentional, like when in our own pain, we say and do things that hurt others.

This is where I was currently residing. In my "passion," my own suffering, I was so much on a crusade that I did not see the collateral damage I was causing—both inside and outside of the Coptic church. A couple of the young people from the Protestant youth group, who were dear to my heart, came to me confused and wounded. They didn't know what to make of years of my teaching and warning about the evils of Roman Catholic beliefs about saints and Mary and confession, now turning around and embracing them. Not only embracing them, but pointing out the ignorance of the Protestants who reject all the beliefs of true Christianity. One precious young lady asked me, "If Protestants aren't Christian, what does that make me?"

I also began to learn that there are many, many blended Orthodox/Protestant families in the Coptic Church. With my cavalier approach, I was only offering the irreconcilable differences between Orthodox Christianity and Protestantism. I offered nothing about how to live in a family with blended faith.

Yet, as I said, we were on a crusade and toured offering a number of talks. One such talk was recorded and posted on YouTube. I was quite concerned as there was a very good chance that if somehow my employer caught wind of it, I could lose my job. Resolute, I resigned myself to; *so be it*. As God wills.

Not long after the talk was posted, something else happened—a dear Protestant friend saw it and was a little shocked and hurt. She confessed that she felt I made something of a joke of Protestants and what they believe. This was someone I cared about and who was genuinely curious about Orthodox Christianity which is why she watched the video to begin with.

As I re-watched the video, this time, not through a self-assessment of was I right and was I engaging, but now, trying to see through her eyes and asking myself if I was kind and loving. The answer was yes to the first, no to the second. We should take very seriously the words of Saint Paul when he said, "Though I speak with the tongues of men and of angels, but have not love,

I have become sounding brass or a clanging cymbal" (I Corinthians 1:3).

Though many said they enjoyed watching the talk, in my spirit I cringe to know this is still out there, and is content Copts consume to learn about Protestantism and Protestants to learn about Orthodoxy. Nevertheless, even in my foolishness, I pray it may be blessed.

I was beginning to become keenly aware of how I was utterly unable to speak about the truth and beauty of Orthodox Christianity without comparing it to how awful and wrong Protestantism is. I was passionate, just as passionate as I was as a Protestant.

Looking back, I would honestly have to say that in those first years, I was still a Protestant who had simply switched theology. In the West, it is sufficient to know and be able to intelligently argue and defend the teaching of the church. In Orthodox Christianity, knowing and understanding the teaching of the Church is incomplete without the spirit of the Church. There is that word again. Worshipping in spirit *and* in truth. But I digress.

In part, my awareness of the skewed theology and intent that is formed into beautiful songs fueled my righteous anger. I could not tolerate love songs to Jesus thanking Him for taking on the wrath and punishment of God. That is *not* the mind of the Church. Still, while I had a glimpse of it, I myself did not have the mind, and truly the heart as well, of my new adoption into the ancient faith. I needed to pump the brakes. Instead of asking permission to be excused from teaching, I began to simply say no. If I didn't come right out and say no, at the very least, I just sat beside my husband as he taught. I offered a tidbit here or there, but as far as

My American Flight to Egypt

I was concerned, for a long time, my teaching days were on hold.[24]

---

[24] Please know that I am not magnifying or diminishing the value of doctrine, theology, or even being passionate. I am simply saying I am convinced I was personally out of balance with truth *and* love.

Chapter 18

> *"'Truly I tell you, unless you...become like little children, you will never enter the Kingdom of heaven.'"*
> Matthew 18:3

Iconic singer/songwriter Bob Dylan has a song called "My Back Pages." One of the many profound verses reads,

"Half-wracked prejudice leaped forth,
'Rip down all hate,' I screamed.
Lies that life is black and white,
Spoke from my skull. I dreamed,
Romantic facts of musketeers,
Foundation-deep, somehow.
Ah, but I was so much older then,
I'm younger than that now."

I love this song because it personifies the immature and untempered zeal we can have when we think we are the only one with clear vision. Look at the lyrics, "'Rip down all hate' I screamed." Does it not drip with contradiction? As did my angry heart when defending truth, entirely forgetting that Truth is a Person, not a proposition—and He is called Love as well. I need you to understand, my convictions have not changed but my heart has. In the lyrics above, the writer hungers to abolish all hate. Is that wrong? No! It is wonderful! But to scream it with anger? That is just adding darkness to darkness. As Abba Isidore demonstrated to Abba Moses the Strong when they sat and watched the sunrise together, light chases away darkness...slowly.

My American Flight to Egypt

There is so much more to unpack in just that small sampling of this powerful song, but here is the biggest take away for me; the line *"Ah, but I was so much older then, I'm younger than that now."* Ten years ago, I fancied myself as wise and knowledgeable—mature if you will. But our Lord calls us to be like little children which, I am learning, does not mean to try to be something you are not, but rather embrace what you truly are. I genuinely do not know much about our Lord, our faith, about people I am judging, what their struggles are. Especially when standing before the Ancient of Days, I am barely an infant, so humility is just and right.

And so it has been the past six or seven years. I have tried to grow into spending less time talking and more time learning. I have sat with the desert fathers and Saint Isaac the Syrian. Then the Russian monk, Saint Theophan the Recluse, and the Serbian Elder Thaddeus. Of course, there was also much to learn from the likes of Saints John Chrysostom, Basil, Cyril, and many others.

Add to those the teachings of some amazing living saints God put in my path who would, in their humility, scold me if they knew I called them saints.

The telling of this story is one decade from my baptism and, even now, I find myself excited about discovering the next thing God will teach me through His Church and His people.

Coming from a young woman who was very uneasy with icons, one would be amused to see our prayer corner at home—even more so in my work office! Yes, I still work for the same Protestant ministry, and have an entire tall bookshelf filled with icons which is the very first thing one sees when entering my office. More than icons—they have become my friends. There is Saint Mary of Egypt and Abba Moses the Strong who teach me the beauty of repentance, Abba Isadore who helped me find a good teacher, Saint Marina who encourages me to humility, then there are Saints Mary Magdalene, Mary and Martha, sisters of Lazarus, George, Peter, even the 21 martyrs of Libya. And any time someone new visits my office, I joyfully introduce them.

Sure. Some people at my job still think I'm a little…different. At the same time, others delight at my daily cheerful greeting of, "*Ya habibi!*"

This ancient faith is simply amazing. A person could never begin to plumb the depths of that which our Lord taught, the disciples preached, and the fathers kept.

It holds everything you could possibly need to know to be united with Christ and healed from brokenness. It has preserved every truth, given us every weapon, and every medicine for the soul. Everything.

I could go on and on, but instead I will pray that our Heavenly Father begins to stoke the flame inside your own heart to go and discover for yourself the treasure hidden in the field.

He so fervently desires for you and I to find this treasure that He has given us the prophets, the martyrs, the confessors, the saints, the apostles, the fathers, the mothers, our clergy, and most of all, the holy virgin, Mother of God, Saint Mary.

He has given us The Church.

Chapter 19

"Jesus did many other things as well. If every one of them were written down, I suppose that even the whole world would not have the room for the books that would be written."

John 21:25

There is much more to this story that could be told if there were time. There were dear Protestant friends who stood close by our side. There were innumerable priests and servants who guided us along the way.

Some of the untold stories would have made you laugh; like when I neglected to make room for an older, full-figured Egyptian woman, and she simply sat on me. Or when I slapped myself in the face in my ignorance of how to take a blessing when kissing a priest's hand and he pulls it away. (Yes. That's a true story.)

You would have also seen God foreshadow Orthodoxy long ago—like while in the Protestant church, I would secretly cover my head during prayer. I wore a scarf on my neck, then would slip it over my head while people's heads were bowed in prayer, then slip it right off again before they opened their eyes so as not to be judged as "legalistic."

You also may have cringed when reading about the times I was a stranger in a Coptic church and looked for a smile, only to be met with stern or suspicious looks.

But mostly, I believe that if you were to have witnessed the entire terrifying, beautiful, amazing journey, you could only glorify God all the more.

The grace of the Lord Jesus Christ, and the love of God, and the communion of the Holy Spirit be with you all. Amen.

Part III: Settling In

Chapter 20

Hi. It's me again. Thilo.

In this section it seems best to abandon the chronological account and move into a topical format. Rather than continuing though the journey, I will speak from the present regarding my own formed views on various subjects I encountered. My intent here is not an exhaustive or scholarly treatment, nor an activist call to change anything for the most part. It is merely to offer things for consideration as seen through the lens of a fairly knowledgeable former Protestant who is very American in his cultural ethos. Perhaps some readers among the clergy and laity may find some value in these points of view as they seek to address the myriad challenges of both the Coptic Orthodox Church here in the West, and Western influences in the Coptic Church in Egypt. I'm certain others have differing yet valid views and emphases. I'm also fairly certain that marry-in converts have very different points of view, and I don't pretend to be able to speak in any way for them (in some cases the "marry-in" does extensive theological investigation, and in those cases I probably see them more as "study-in").

In some of these matters I speak from what I gather to be a fairly unique perspective, in others from a broadly shared view among former Protestants who were also well-studied prior to conversion, most being now in other Orthodox jurisdictions.

In all matters I hope to come across as I am: one who can see and acknowledge some problems in this Coptic/American culture clash while also maintaining a deep love for these Coptic

Orthodox people who, being in many ways very other, me neither needing nor desiring to place anyone in black-and-white categories, are dearly loved and embraced as my chosen family of faith. We are all mixtures, and some things which are good and needed in one context can be less useful or even problematic in another.

Above all, I hope to inspire Copts to truly see and appreciate their own religious heritage; one often taken for granted or even looked at with some mild disdain by some whom I believe lack perspective. I hope to remain sympathetic in my criticisms to some of the problems of being a child of an immigrant, being one myself. In the world of the young, fitting in is paramount, and having had a mother who was very much other, I too wanted nothing more than to shed any differences between me and my peers. As I grew to understand, appreciate, and even embrace some of the cultural differences with which I was brought up in my later adult life, and at minimum I started to understand the hardships and context of her own history. This in turn caused me to love and appreciate her more prior to her passing. I hope some younger Copts will also come to see their elders in a more fitting and appreciative light. They really are quite remarkable.

Too often is it the case that in seeing problems and errors, those younger and zealous ones, for noble reasons, inadvertently throw out many treasures which took generations to acquire while thinking they are cleaning house. Such I believe was sadly the case during the Protestant Reformation of the West and is the tendency during times of change. The need for careful inquiry and understanding how things came to be and what needs they serve(d), being careful to preserve the good, is the difference between mere change, in which problems are simply replaced by other problems, perhaps worse, and actual improvement.

With this in mind, I'll begin the next chapter with an excerpt from an article I wrote for a Coptic parish magazine some years ago.

Chapter 21

"Therefore, since we are surrounded by so great a cloud of witnesses, let us also lay aside every weight, and sin which clings so closely, and let us run with endurance the race that is set before us, looking to Jesus, the founder and perfecter of our faith, who for the joy that was set before him endured the cross, despising the shame, and is seated at the right hand of the throne of God."
Hebrews 12:1-2

An American Viewpoint of an Egyptian Mother

I hear much talk about people, mostly young ones, leaving the church. I read and participated in an exchange recently where a priest was asking why others believed this was happening. What was making them leave? I would like to offer some thoughts in answer to this question.

It has been rightly said by Saint Cyprian that the Church is our mother and God is our Father. Well, the part of mother Copts get to see, happens to be Egyptian, meaning: she is always in our business; telling us what path to take; unwilling to change the things that brought her through troubles and suffering that we, in our young lives, have not experienced. She is bossy and controlling.

Well, that is how she is often seen by her children, who grew up in her house.

But I would like to tell you about our mother from the perspective of my wife and I. I'm sure we are considered "the Americans" and seem to be somewhat unique in this as neither of us married into this family. We were adopted, so to speak. No Egyptian friends, family, spouse, nothing—total strangers.

We came from the American Evangelical background, where my wife says, "Churches are like girlfriends. No need to commit. When things don't go well, you leave, go down the street to another one, and start again there."

For us, as adopted kids entering into an Egyptian home with an Egyptian mother, things look quite different. We are in awe. Mother is nosy, yes. But it is only because she loves us. She is old and wise, and knows the suffering we can bring on ourselves by wrong choices. She tries to protect us and steer us to the path of peace and safety. She bears not only her wisdom, but the wisdom of the entire family through the centuries. She suffers when we suffer. She cleans and bandages our wounds. She feeds us. She clothes us in humility. All this can seem like a controlling old mom to many who have never been an orphan, who have always lived this way, but to us, she is a treasure unlike any we have known.

And yes, the deep scars she bears after keeping the faith through persecution and mistreatment, a suffering which would have stopped the moment she was willing to abandon her family, but never even considered it as she is a faithful mother, can show sometimes. She's not perfect, but she is beautiful. Her dress is soaked with the tears of seeing her children abused and killed for belonging to her family—the stains of those tears make her dress more beautiful than the finest silk in all the world.

It took several years for the community at Saint John to truly welcome us as their own, though from the beginning Abouna Daniel was a trusted friend and spiritual adviser. A few younger Copts welcomed and helped us through the liturgy. Other than that, we were outsiders. But it didn't matter. I was a tattooed biker American wearing a tee-shirt to church. I knew I didn't fit in. I quickly learned of the suffering and deep faith of the Copts, and figured such persecution knits a people together closely, and probably makes them cautious of outsiders. I was partaking of a treasure paid for and preserved by the blood of their parents, and I was grateful.

I suppose it may be because word got back to them that I was not there to change them, or that I was zealous with love for this church, or that I sought to humble myself under them, or that I became a servant at times—I don't know. But after a few years I began to be embraced. Not just by the American born, but by the Egyptians who didn't even speak English. The ones who never smiled began smiling at me. And it meant more to me than all the warm welcomes I received at all the American churches I ever attended. It was something not given lightly or cheaply.

I'd like to challenge all the young, American-born Copts: first, seek God. He is here. And if nobody else ever was kind to you, or ever treated you like you think you should be treated, that should be enough.

I'd like to challenge you to see the good, as we did. Of course, there are hypocrites, those who don't live this faith as it should be, but you don't know why, and it doesn't matter anyway. I heard it said that a hummingbird seeks life and a buzzard seeks death. And they both find what they seek. In every parish there are those to whom you can point and say "that's what it should look like!" Fix your eyes on them.

See your Abouna. We quickly learned that probably because of 2,000 years of tending to persecuted sheep the Coptic priests are among the best in the world. Seek them out. Ask them for guidance. Listen to them and do as they say. Even if they make a mistake, the blessing from God will be yours simply because of the humility of obedience. Our Abouna taught us, baptized us, chrismated us, married us in the church, and gave us our first communion on Easter. And to see his gentle smile when he prays over us the absolution is to see Christ. Nothing in the world (take it from one that has taken more of what the world has to offer than I care to admit) can equal his role in our lives and salvation. Your Abouna can be the same for you if you only seek it with sincerity and diligence.

Have compassion for your elders. You'll never know the things they went through. But this you do know: they are among the 10-15% of all Egypt who kept the faith—who carried it on—who suffered for it. And if they err, or if there is something you see that should be changed, ask yourself, "What am I doing with what I have? They did this under suffering, but what shall I do with my freedom? I have access to knowledge they never dreamed possible. I have nobody persecuting me. How can I do as much with this as they did with their circumstance?"

What excuse will we have before the Judgment Seat of Christ? Shall we stand next to the woman with the issue of blood (Mark 5:25-34) who fought through the crowds, being unclean, to touch the hem of His garment and say, "Well, I abandoned the faith because someone was mean to me?" Shall we stand next to Blind Bartimaeus (Mark 10:46-52) whom they could not silence, but shouted even louder, "Have mercy on me!" and say, "I let you pass by because someone didn't treat me as I thought they should?" Shall we stand among the countless martyrs whose lives were demanded because of their faithfulness to the church and say, "I left the church, but I still kept my faith?" Shall we stand before our King who was crucified and say, "It was too hard?"

If we see something lacking, it is for us to add it, not to abandon the very place we believe needs it. It is for you, the young, to add what this new land needs to be able to experience the unique beauty of the Coptic Church—not to criticize the elders who have run their race and kept the faith. It is for you to keep and preserve the spirit of humility, deep and quiet faith, silent suffering, and simple hope that has been at the heart of the Coptic Church for millennia.

You have been handed a baton in a race. It is covered with the blood of Christ, the Apostles, the martyrs, and your ancestors. God forbid you should throw it in the dirt and leave the race! Carry it, preserve the good, change in yourselves the things that may not be perfect, and add to it what is needed in this place. And in time, you too will pass it on.

Chapter 22

"Therefore humble yourselves under the mighty hand of God, that He may exalt you in due time, casting all your care upon Him, for He cares for you."
1 Peter 5:6-7

Two Types of Spirituality

One of the first differences in common vocabulary usage I encountered was our Protestant phrase "going to church." We say "praying" in Orthodox parlance. For instance, we Orthodox don't ask, "Where do you go to church?" but, "Where do you pray?" And that difference is not merely one of terminology; it is substantial. The overwhelming majority of the Orthodox liturgy is in fact quite literally prayer. Communal prayer.

While a relatively small portion of the time of assembly is the homily, such is only done on Sundays (or the Saturday morning gathering held in some parishes which can be an optional alternative to the Sunday gathering), which is significant when one considers how frequently liturgies are held (at least Sunday, Wednesday and Friday, with often another day also) in most parishes, and daily liturgies available in many places during the fifty-five days of Lent/Holy Week. Besides this homily, the time of readings (without commentary) is the only other substantial time of the liturgy when someone is standing facing the people and speaking. (Oddly, as a *Sola scriptura* Evangelical, I was given a few verses accompanied by forty or so minutes of opinion commentary, while now in a church often criticized for not having enough Bible, I get chapters with no opinion added as the norm). The rest of the time everyone is facing the Altar, praying. Of course, this is with the exception of the final culmination of the liturgy when we all go forward to receive Christ into our bodies and join with Him and one another in communion. At that time, we are facing the Body and Blood of Christ.

The brunt of the Orthodox spiritual life (in terms of time invested) occurs away from church. While under the individual guidance of a spiritual father, we are given rules, or spiritual disciplines, which generally center around prayers, scriptural and spiritual reading and fasting. I can well understand the revulsion of my western Evangelical friends at such an idea. We Americans do not like constraints to our autonomy. We *hate* being told what to do.

I have been asked a number of times, "What did you like about Orthodoxy?" or, "What drew you to Orthodoxy?" Such questions I presumed to be based on the overwhelmingly common form of choosing a spiritual path: resonance. In other words, "What was it about this that you found sufficiently appealing to make you 'buy in' so to speak?" I usually answer, "There are a lot of things I really hate," in an effort to begin to turn the discussion to an objective one of truth, rather than the subjective experience of a religion shopper who seeks the *just right* fit and style to compliment his tastes.

I explain how the necessity of confessing my humiliating sins to someone, and worse yet the same ones *every* darn time, to have rules and long liturgies, can be tormenting. While the spiritual tools of Orthodoxy are of course prescriptive, in giving us a well-proven path to spiritual growth, they are also descriptive, forcing us to face ourselves, our own weaknesses and sicknesses of the heart.

I never really understood the extent of my ego until I was in a place of subjection to someone else. What makes it worse is my awareness that this priest is entirely sympathetic and always on my side, yet I still have this tendency to dislike being instructed and subjecting myself to him. Likewise, my embarrassment in speaking to him of the things I seemed to have no shame doing right in front of God expose some ego and faith problems I don't like seeing.[25]

I never understood how uncommitted I was until I found myself unable to give my heart and mind to God for a few hours on Sunday, finding myself drifting off into thoughts of things I need to do or what to have for lunch. And it gets worse! The daily prayer rule! One of the Hours of Prayer takes between ten and twenty minutes to complete, on average. To be incapable of sustaining this daily practice, to have my thoughts drift as I try, exposes the lack of control I have over my own mind, as well as my lack of true heartfelt commitment towards God.

The fasting rule speaks to me of my belly as my master.

My inability to sit in silent introspection before the candles and icons in my prayer corner, instead having my mind race in a hundred directions, speaks to the hidden things of the heart from which I run, not wanting to face them and the ramifications of seeing myself truly.

---

[25] I heard many Protestants speak of going only to God, and not a man, with their sins as being more noble. I try to point out the reality of the situation by asking them about viewing pornography or some other hidden sin, "Have you ever or would you ever do it in front of your pastor? Why not? Yet we do it in front of God. What does that tell us?"

All these things are crushing, yet essential in diagnosing and treating the spiritual sickness in me. They are humiliating, painful, and necessary, yet some of the basic practices of Orthodox spiritual life.

Unlike the juridical view of salvation of the western Evangelical churches, in which the basic issue is one of retributive justice, in which someone needs to suffer torment and death in order to appease God's sense of justice, wherein Jesus steps in to take our place, we having faith and trust in what He did, exonerating us from culpability for our sins (and the required retributive torments), resolving the legal issues, we Orthodox understand things in an ontological way.

While the needed change in the state of being is accomplished by God at death with an instant *poof*, rendering us now perfect (at the time of the *sinner's prayer* we are understood to have been made spiritually perfect, while nonetheless physically fallen, creating a rather dual state) and no longer desiring to sin (to which one ought to ask, "Why not just make us that way in the first place?") in this recent Western theology, in the Orthodox Churches the change of state of being (ontology) is quite literally essential to our ongoing participation (synergy) in salvation here and now; not an event but a process, in which the event is the starting line, not the finish line. And this process is understood in terms of healing what went wrong in us in the first place.

Man is seen as a psychosomatic unity that was fragmented into a tripartite being, his original hierarchy being led by the superiority of his heart being fashioned in the image of God. This fragmented being, albeit still operating simultaneously yet somehow paradoxically. His highest faculties of the heart or the spirit (nous) deliberating, deciding, directing, and communicating with God. The soul perceiving, having instincts and impulses. Finally, the body having the sensory perceptions and physical desires. This proper order was reversed at the fall of man, salvation ultimately being restoration to proper order and completion of his highest state, Christ being the prototype. Unlike "making someone suffer as retribution," the term "justification" is seen as properly meaning "setting things as they ought to be." Ordering the chaos.

Therefore, the process of uncovering the sickness in us, as well as healing it, are primary components of the Orthodox spiritual life. The pathetic, broken weakness in us being revealed is essential to the repentance which enables the healing, growth, and proper union with/orientation towards God. The two approaches, being grounded in different premises, are naturally quite disharmonious.

Say you have a pain. Unknown to you, it is cancer. And there are two doctors, each educated differently and each being benevolent and sincere in their intentions.

The first doctor will give you pain killers. You'll feel great in forty-five minutes. Sure, the pain will return in a few hours, but he gives you enough to keep the pain at bay, and take another pill each time it rises back up. He pronounces you cured, and you definitely feel cured. This is all he really knows about medicine, and did his best. Your sensory experience is his gauge for your well-being.

The second gives you bad news. Your condition will be terminal if left untreated. What's worse, he's going to put you through much more pain than you experience now. He's going to cause your hair to fall out, make you sick, cut you open, remove tissue, and overall put you through hell. He understands the extent of the disease and its dangers, and knows this is the only way to make you truly healthy again. His gauge is an awareness of the proper state of your physical being.

When one is done, you'll be dead from the cancer, but felt better for your remaining time. When the other is done, you'll have gone through a horrible ordeal, but will emerge healthy and lead a long and joyous life. Those are your options.

Having spent some years in a nationally televised church, I was given the best of the best of Contemporary Christian Worship. Professional musicians, high quality singers, top-notch performance. I can't begin to express how disheartening it is to walk into a Coptic youth meeting and hear poorly (relatively) performed renditions of what I chose to leave behind. And not, for the most part, due to the poor performance quality, certainly not for lack of good intent, but much more so because being born of a very different religion (I'll go into how I have come to sort through what the differences between Orthodoxy and Protestantism mean regarding the question, "Can they both be the Church?" further down) the two are, again, simply disharmonious.

The Hebrew and Greek terms for worship are derived from "work." Literal work. It is work performed for the greater One. While the work is part of the restoration of our proper order of being, the immediate fulfillment of the one working is not the point. While there is a longer-term fulfillment of the desire to be free from the inherited human sickness of sin and its ramifications, such a cure can only be administered by the True Physician. Our part is to be the willing and obedient patient who shows up for his treatment and follows His guidance.

The Orthodox life is one of self-emptying, not self-fulfillment. Denying the driving forces which demand immediate gratification, not feeding them. The intent is to put the passions of the flesh to death, relegating it to subjection where it now has mastery, which is a long and painful process. The symbol is Jesus on a cross, not in a lounge chair. It is a well-established ancient process of removing and healing sickness, of deliberate and sober movement which requires a continuous effort and daily repentance. It is certainly not for the faint of heart; similar to the difference between an immediate sugar rush and the health experienced by one who follows a careful regimen of nutrition and exercise.

Conversely, having secured Heaven at the time of a recited prayer at an altar call, while obtaining virtues is desirable, generally understood in the context of being a more moral person, it's not truly essential to our salvation in modern Western Christian religions. This is not to say that morality is not a common or even central theme to many in the Evangelical West, and certainly not to say that there aren't countless wonderfully moral people, but rather to point out that being depicted as a natural result, rather than something we sacrificially struggle towards as an essential aspect of salvation itself, it is more or less *optional*. It is faith alone which gets you to heaven.

For all practical purposes, the emphasis easily lands on the now, this life. Relationships, work, and practical "how to" sermons about living your best life take the place of ancient self-emptying spirituality, sermons now being delivered too often by sermon performers rather than spiritual guides. In fact, I seem to recall some Bible translation using the term *asceticism* in place of *false humility*, so as to associate ascetical practice with a vice rather than spiritual growth.[26]

It is important to note here that for most adherents of the tens of thousands of modern Western schisms there is nothing nefarious going on, a few hucksters here and there notwithstanding. In fact, particularly having large numbers of converts and/or church hoppers, they can tend to have many of the more sincere and zealous congregations. One usually goes from church to church because one is seeking something more. There is a yearning and a sense of something missing that keeps them searching. I have a deep love for these people. Indeed, among those who do yearn and strive for something more, the tools available are scant, the guidance is poor (the individual guidance by a selected spiritual father being virtually non-existent, it is usually peer groups, all members being equally ill-equipped for the most part, to which they turn for help in small groups), and the two-thousand-year history of luminaries and ascetics is unknown.

I have often said that in Orthodoxy we have a banquet table of teachings, practices, and disciplines that few will ever consume, even if they moved to the desert, abandoned their jobs and worldly pursuits, and devoted themselves completely to God. Our priests will guide us into what to eat from the seemingly endless supply of spiritual nutrition stored up in the church, helping us to know when and how much to eat, keeping us struggling in our movement toward holiness while not overburdening us into discouragement. There is a fine line here requiring the sort of trust and expertise which simply cannot be found in a small group of laity. On the other hand, as a Protestant,

---

[26] Colossians 2:18, 23 (ESV).

I was told to pray and read my Bible. Fasting was almost never mentioned. But how much do I do this? How can I know when I'm on track and sufficiently struggling, or reaching too far in my pride, and when I'm being a lazy slacker? I was pretty much on my own, and the concept of a community-shared pursuit of spiritual growth through seasons of shared practice was virtually non-existent.

Here I must make an important distinction: when people hear me criticize modern Western Christian religion, it is understandable that they mistake that criticism for disdain for the people. But it's simply not true, and I want that to be very clear here. By and large they are good people seeking Christ, and I daresay they can tend to be more zealous and dedicated than many cradle Orthodox. More and more, in their pursuit of God, almost all I know through that pursuit leading to an inquiry into church history, I see Protestants coming to discover the Orthodox Church. The infusion of their zeal with the stability and deep ethos of an Orthodox community can be most complimentary, provided a good priest and mentor is present to steer and curtail the excess zeal, turning a wildfire into a deliberate and useful "slow burn" (they're still working on tamping mine down, and God willing it will happen someday), as my dear Protestant friend Brian puts it.

All that to say this: good and honest people who take for granted as true what they are taught, who have never been introduced to a true understanding of the ancient churches, but are pursuing truth as best they can, ought to be respected and embraced for the posture of zeal and sincerity they possess. And it is usually to our embarrassment that they've never even heard of the Orthodox Faith, though they are our neighbors. While our ethos is so strongly focused on both a personal and corporate quiet spiritual development, including vital virtues, perhaps a bit of attention to evangelism may well be in order. Yes, we are to live the faith, but maybe it is okay to speak it too?

I'm sure some readers will rightly note the conversions which happen the other way—from Orthodoxy to Protestantism, but I would offer this observation: while many notable Protestant scholars and theologians have become Orthodox, I have yet to hear of any Orthodox scholars or theologians becoming Protestant. I believe there's a good reason why.

Most conversions rooted in knowledge (as opposed to shoppers simply finding the alternate product more personally appealing) occur when new, factual information is obtained. But for the Orthodox scholar or theologian, there's really nothing new to be heard from Protestantism. He knows his Bible. He knows his church history and is steeped in it. He understands and possesses a coherent theology which he can trace back to the earliest centuries of his faith.

On the other hand, for the Protestant it's almost always new information regarding church history which proves to be the turning point. They discover the early Church and, in that pursuit, find themselves amazed to realize it still exists. Usually there is an element of resonance, admittedly, regarding what they felt was lacking but hadn't yet truly identified. There had been a sense for quite some time that the Evangelical religion is somewhat shallow, trite, and consumerist. They had a sense that it should just have a more sacred and holy feel.

While resonance does tend to play a role in each case, I can say that I've never spoken to one former Orthodox who converted to Protestantism who possessed an even moderate level of understanding of their own prior faith. They tend to be generally less knowledgeable than an average Orthodox catechumen, and simply find the religion of their neighbors more appealing personally. While a few parishes have sought to keep them by adding the neighboring religion's materials and practices to the Orthodox faith, I find this a tragic and dangerous error. Proper education would be a much more fitting answer. Yes, this is a call to some improved form of general catechesis for all the Orthodox, not just converts. Proper understanding is essential.

I remember, during my catechesis, attending a Protestant baptism for the wife of a dearly beloved friend. The sermon was about guilt. The pastor passionately chided those who bore painful guilt as, "not truly believing in the finished work of Christ to forgive your sins." The guilt, as he understood it, was the result of a lack of faith.

I was literally squirming in my seat, both angry and heartbroken. I saw people who were suffering under the weight of their sins, now being chastised by a church who had thrown out the ancient and established means of addressing the sins accumulated after baptism: the Sacrament of Confession. My heart was breaking for them, knowing their sense of guilt was valid, and their desire to be free from it was good, yet the very means of doing so had been removed. They knew their feet were dirty and needed to be washed—they could see it—but he was telling them they just needed to trust that they were clean.

I should note that the recently developed small group settings often have accountability to one another, which does serve as a pseudo-confession of sorts, yet lacking the guidance of an ordained expert spiritual mentor, instead being guided by the rest of the group which is just as unlearned as the one being guided, and with no guarantee of privacy, I think you can see the inherent issues. Further, there is no person in authority to pronounce an absolution. The need seems to be tacitly known, yet not properly identified or addressed.

Amid the Western Reformation efforts was a sentiment of rejection of all things Rome,[27] which lingers to this day. While there were certainly legitimate grievances regarding the frequent corruption, I believe the empty religious experience observed by those zealous for something profound and substantial was, and is, at the forefront. Indeed to this day, modern Western Christians refer to the Roman Church as "dead religion." I suppose it's inherent in any traditional religion for people to drift into a vacuous repetition of the form while having little to no personal commitment or zeal, no understanding of the substance beneath that form. We see this pattern in the Old Testament a generation or two after God would deliver the sincere and desperate people from peril, as a recurrent theme. Soon it became rote and they would look to the religion of the neighboring peoples to spice things up a bit, or relegate thoughts of God to the prescribed times of ordered religious duty, then go back about the business of obtaining their desires with no further mind of Him.

Yet God, who delivered and instituted this ritualistic and tightly structured worship system, never, ever saw it in need of "revamping" in order to address this repeated tendency toward stale religious practice.

He always seemed to point to the same thing: your heart.

Certainly, the communal and sacramental nature of the ancient faith can easily have a tendency toward a hat-tip of empty religious observance by people relying on the institution, membership, and sacraments to save them, to the abandonment of the deep personal involvement and commitment. I think if we

---

[27] I have come to use the term "Romophobia" as a fitting description.

are honest, we can admit this to be the case far too often in our own churches today, as well as our individual lives. The call of God to "teach your children" and to continue to struggle and self-examine personally could not be more important to the Copts than it is today.

We need to understand what it all means, its profundity and relevance to daily life, rather than trying to spice it up, which only works for a short time anyway. While we may find instances of something new being of value to jump start us, these experiences cannot sustain us. It will always come down to the will. The decision. The sacrifice. The deliberate focus. The direction of the heart.

I would argue that the proneness to a descent into cold ritual speaks to our sickness, not to a failure of the system. And in doing so, it exposes us to ourselves, if we are willing, and so brings us face to face with our own lack of a sober and decided will towards the things of God. Exciting and constant newness actually prevents us from seeing and addressing this issue of the heart, just as a pain killer keeps us from any acute awareness of the symptoms of a disease.

Having overcome persecution, discrimination, and every sort of hardship, the one test that Copts have rarely experienced, if ever, is perhaps the most potentially deadly to a church: freedom and prosperity.

Here in the West, that test is in full force. Your children are being pulled from all sides. From atheist professors at universities and their wide-eyed student disciples who seek to be among the intellectually advanced, looking down on the religious simpletons, to the constant bombardment of advertisements feeding materialistic desires, to a sexually obsessed culture; all these play together quite nicely as enticements to the children of immigrants who just want to fit in, whose home has emphasized and reinforced education and career to such an effective level of personal success that they can in fact have all these things they are told by this new culture to want. Their general career success is quite impressive, yet can be most dangerous to the spiritual life. Scarcely do they have the understanding of their own religion to protect them from such assaults when they are vulnerable. We certainly have a need for quality apologetics and deeper theological education here in the American experience of the Coptic diaspora.[28]

Having a deep disdain for this apparently empty ritual form of religion in the Catholic West, the Reformers and after took the pendulum and swung it to the other extreme. Two things which ought to properly be held in harmony and balance were, in the neglect of the one, turned into an abandonment of the other.

The sacraments on which people relied for salvation were relegated to mere symbol as the pursuit of the individual commitment of the heart, which had been neglected, became the center. Indeed, a common battle cry is, "Relationship, not religion!"

Salvation of the community, together, was de-emphasized in favor of the personal decision and individual (often romanticized) relationship with Christ.

---

[28] I am in no way criticizing the lack of apologetics and theological knowledge in those immigrating from Egypt. What is very important here need not be seen as nearly so urgent in their prior context, although with the introduction of the Internet perhaps that context is now changing.

The Sacrament of Baptism as entry into Christ was replaced by the personal prayer of acceptance of His efforts to save you. In short, believing and trusting alone.

Works were set in opposition to faith, and deemed by many at times even evil to pursue if understood as having a salvific intent.

The Church, as a structured institution, eventually became the object of disdain, along with any central authority, which concept is a repugnant idea in such liberty-minded, autonomous people as Americans.

Everything became deeply individual and personal, to the exclusion of the communal.

Not surprisingly, the music later emerging reflected and conveyed this theology. Many cradle Coptic Orthodox, judging Christian music by lyrical content alone, not finding direct heresies, are shocked to be introduced to the idea that musical style is theological. It reflects and conveys ethos, and ethos is an unspoken summary of the entire faith. The historical faith's music was chant. It conveyed the deep, sacred, and solemn. It was never intended to invoke and manipulate emotions, as the immediate satisfaction of the worshiper was never the primary intent of it in the first place. Offering to God was. It was something far less "goose-bumpy" and far more sober and profound. It's not as though emotions are taboo in Orthodoxy, but rather that they are not the goal. They are a frequent byproduct, as we worship with the whole person- mind, body and spirit- but we are (or ought to be) acutely aware that such experiences are not indicators of spiritual growth.

Modern Christian music is not coincidentally of the style and lyrical content of a romantic song conveying a newfound "puppy love." After all, it's about a hyper-emphasis on a personal relationship with the One who loves me, and as such, drifting into a clear romantic theme is probably inevitable.

Unfortunately, as in the relationships of teenagers, and sadly too many adults, when the warm fuzzy feelings wear off, as they inevitably do, something new is needed or people will leave. Hence the song life in an Evangelical Church being a couple months or so (just as the themed sermon series which gets hyped up as "life changing" requires a constant newness). Not coincidentally, as I understand it, these modern innovations were first implemented in an attempt to keep younger kids from leaving the churches of the West. They were literally the juvenilization of the faith. But alas, the deep and lifelong devotional love of a teenager fades quicky.

Then we need a new "high." Again, enter the pain killers.

As my wife once quipped seeing yet another hyped-up advertisement of yet another revival, "If it needs to be revived that much, maybe you should just let it die." Harsh joking aside, her remark was poignant. Something vital and healthy ought to not need you to constantly break out the defibrillator.

But here is the biggest danger I see.

Anyone who has done a deep Lent, with the food abstinence, increased prayers, increased scripture and spiritual readings, increased liturgy attendance, shutting down entertainment and all media, including Internet, and devoted themselves to the arduous process of emptying the self to make room for God, while focusing daily attentions on Him, all with the continued guidance of a priest, has probably come to understand true Orthodox spirituality, at least on some level. The deep peace which is not the same as happiness, which is rather superficial by comparison, the "bright sadness" described by Schmemann,[29] mixing sorrow over sins and the state of the world with a deep reverential joy at seeing the hand of God in it all as He opens the eyes, with the joy and sorrow over His sacrifice for us, and the very sober reflective state, becomes (or ought to) the framework of understanding the spiritual life.

While I believe the criticisms of the older religions to be valid in their notice of a lack of personal relationship among many adherents, I also believe that when one discovers the truest applications and understandings of the Orthodox Faith, one comes to an understanding of a much more profound level of relationship than the modern Western faiths afford. The practices of self-emptying and self-examination, if entered into with all sincerity and zeal, strip away the layers of facade, removing the cumulative debris of things collected around our hearts in our fallenness, and open the way to a rich, deep and pure relationship, which I believe to be infinitely more authentic than a mere sentimental emotionality. The depth of relationship cannot be separated from the authenticity of the true human: the one who has returned to his primordial state. As we strip away the sickness, so we become the true self. And any relationship is contingent on the true self, as otherwise it would be a relationship with some other which is not truly "self."

Yet for so many this is simply too much effort, or they've never even understood why they ought to do so. They never experience it because they never find the will or wisdom to give up all they must to obtain it. Sadly some Copts, not understand this and going to Evangelical popular preachers for religio-

---

[29] See Alexander Schmemann, *For the Life of the World: Sacraments and Orthodoxy*, (Yonkers: St. Vladimir's Seminary Press, 1997).

entertainment as a substitute, usually criticizing their own faith, which they don't quite understand, as being stale or unappealing.

So comes the pain killer in lieu of the life-saving treatment and surgeries. We can obtain a pseudo-spirituality in three songs, without all the introspection and long periods of committed sacrifice. When we have assuaged the pain, we have removed much of the incentive to seek treatment. In fact, we in the West underestimate the value of pain as a driving force for incentive for personal change. We see all pain, all discomfort, as something inherently bad and needing to be removed, when it is in fact the suffering of sin and its effects which has always been a primary driver of men to seek God, or even change in general. If a man cuts off his hand, pain killers will make him feel better while he dies of blood loss.

The worst part is it is believed to be spirituality! It's not that I am anti-emotion. However, I sense a very real danger in mistaking fleeting emotions for spiritual growth and maturity. I mean, who seeks after what they already possess? Why pay that price when you can have it in fifteen or twenty minutes with the help of a good band and moving singer (not to mention smoke machines and a light show! All we have is a censor and candles)? My wife and I would be the biggest fools of all. We gave up so much and brought many past and ongoing struggles and hardships on ourselves for nothing if we already had it. But we now understand the difference, and that we had was not this, but a rather shallow recent American innovation made to appeal to an insatiable consumerist culture which has no interest in true sacrifice, self-examination, or worst of all, disciplines. We want it now. We want it cheap. We buy things that make us feel good, not crosses.

These modern innovations are not new because nobody in two thousand years had the brilliance of insight to commission contemporary pop music as a vehicle for faith. It's because they weren't after fleeting emotional highs, but God. They understood the difference between emotion and spirituality. And they had generations of luminaries who gave up all they had to find Him, leaving us a roadmap.

Orthodox spirituality isn't cheap. It is quite literally a cross. And it isn't designed to immediately elevate you emotionally, nor to take you to the top of the mountain and offer you the world. It isn't intended to lift you up in that way. In fact, it's much the opposite. It's to bring you down, in humble submission and self-emptying, elevating Him, and in losing your life, there and only there, to find it. We empty, with His help, and He fills. Our efforts are not on His part, but ours. His lifting isn't our part, but His.

Chapter 23

"Therefore, brethren, stand fast and hold the traditions which you were taught, whether by word or our epistle."
2 Thessalonians 2:15

Aren't We All Christians?

Amid my rather sharp, at times, criticisms of Protestant beliefs and practices (which of course flow naturally from beliefs), I think most people believe they know how I view people of my former religion. But they are probably wrong.

As previously noted, I have a great love and respect for the zeal and dedication of many evangelical Protestants. Mostly they are just seeking God. However, I simply feel I have no right to redefine established language.

The term "Christian" was first established in Antioch in the first century (Acts 11:26). It referred to a specific religious group with specific beliefs and practices. I have come to the conclusion that this ancient, liturgical, sacramental religion, with its established succession of authority, is distinct and separate from the churches established during the Reformation, as well as their countless splinters. The beliefs and practices are just too disparate to call them the "same", and since this term is long established and held by the Apostolic Churches, I simply don't think I have the right to apply it in some new way. This isn't about my views, as I seek constantly to subject them to those of the historical Church, but the long-held language of those who preserved and passed down this faith to me.

Similarly, I hear Copts refer to Protestants as brothers. But this is, biblically and historically, a term of ontological reference. This language referred to one who was *born* into this family, became a member of the Body of Christ through baptism and chrismation in the ancient and continuous Church. It is quite literally a statement of one's state of being. And as such, I don't think I have the right to apply it to those outside the Apostolic Churches. Imagine someone starting a new church down the street from the one Saint Paul established in Corinth, having a self-appointed authority and claiming autonomy from the existing one. Now imagine they also rejected such central beliefs as those surrounding baptism and the sacraments. Would the Apostles have acknowledged that as part of the Church?

I believe terms like "believers in Christ" or "God-fearers" to be more appropriate, when speaking in exacting terms.

You see, for me to use the other long-established language in this new way would be to infer claims I simply do not believe I have the right to make. While some, I know, point to the dogma from the councils of the early centuries as defining the parameters of what it is to be a Christian, I believe this form of measurement is an errant view of the councils. These established terms of dogma, these specifically worded definitions, were never intended to offer a comprehensive delineation of what is required in terms of belief to be properly called "Christian" or "member of the Church." Rather, they were explanations of what is required belief *regarding some debated point of controversy*. Things like the ever-virginity of Saint Mary, the real presence of the Body and Blood, the efficacy of baptism, etc., were never questioned. Nobody challenged such established and universal beliefs, therefore there was no need to define essentials in these matters. I have no doubt as to how the universal Church would have responded to rejections of these basics.

The closest parallel I can find to groups who claim to be the real church, existing apart from those established by the Apostles, having no succession of authority, who reject the sacraments, and having beliefs that radically separate the physical from the spiritual, would be the Gnostics. And we know how the Church defined them. They weren't heretics because they never had been part of the Church. They were simply another religion which was trying to co-opt the faith, redefine it, and claim it as their own. In opposition to the Gnostic claims of "secret teachings handed down to the elites, which were above the ability of the masses to accept or understand", the early Christians simply said "they aren't a part of us, and they never were. And they're wrong."

But what of my experiences as a Protestant?

One major dilemma I faced upon becoming Orthodox in my heart and mind, before baptism, was the question of past experiences with God. What was that? How do I categorize them and what was I if not a Christian, properly speaking? As noted earlier, if you asked me to say, then or now, that what I experienced was not God, I couldn't do it. I know it was. But how can that be if I wasn't properly "in Christ" or part of the Church?

The quandary was based on a premise: one's access to and interaction with, indeed one's ultimate salvific status in God, is based on believing the right things. But is that correct? I reflected back on my time as a Protestant, and noted how I had changed in some very important areas of belief (good grief, the cornucopia of offerings of points of view regarding various theological beliefs is almost endless), and experienced God in each. Could it be that affirming the correct facts was not the be-all end-all? Was I missing something? I believe I was.

One of the unanswered questions I see in the early Church was, "how much can someone sin after baptism and still be saved?" They all seemed to believe there was a point of no return, yet there seemed to be no final settling answer to what that was. It appears that the Apostles only said, "Walk here if you want to get to God," and never told us how far we could stray and still arrive at the destination. If they did, we would probably be walking with that line in mind, rather than the one they gave us.

"Walk here."

"How far can I stray though?"

"I SAID WALK HERE!"

While we were given a roadmap, we were never told how far we can deviate. And we ALL deviate. We all depart the path and return to it when we sin and repent. Unlike the "Sinner's Prayer" line of "saved versus damned" in my prior faith, things aren't so black-and-white here. We are all seen as being on a path, a common saying being, "God will judge us all based on what we did with the light we had." Indeed, much like Saint Justin Martyr's use of the "seminal Logos" (the seeds of the Word which can be found everywhere throughout history as men understood various things about Christ), each man has some level of awareness of God, and responds differently to the light he receives. When we say "we can't judge (regarding ultimate states, *not* regarding issues of right and wrong, as some have misapplied this axiom), we mean it. Such judgments belong to the hidden things of God.

Nonetheless, we Orthodox believe we have been given the most complete and comprehensive knowledge of God in Christ, and a sure path to His eternal Kingdom. And this is where we are taught to struggle to walk. Yet of those outside, we cannot say, except to affirm that one only comes to Christ through the Holy Spirit's guidance and their affirmative response. And that interaction and relationship precedes and leads to the very baptism we (adults) receive. So, it seems we can hear from God, interact with Him, be blessed by Him, while being yet, properly speaking, "outside the Church," and the terms of the continued guidance and interaction do seem to be tied most closely with one's posture in seeking with humility and sincerity, not through merely affirming the correct set of propositions. We need not reject the notion that one can clearly be in relationship with God as they seek Him to the best of their ability while yet not properly being called Christian, by the historical use of the term.

I quite simply have no right to redefine the parameters or meanings of what was handed down.

Chapter 24

Struggle

As an American convert, of course there have been difficulties for me at times. In no particular order, I would like to discuss some of these here.

The Loss

If you notice, we humans tend to congregate around common interests, in groups. From motorcycle riders to fishermen to collector clubs to political affiliation to bowling to countless other areas of pursuit. It's not surprising that we gravitate towards like-minded people.

Well, for a great many of us who find Orthodoxy through a zealous religious pursuit which eventually takes us to the historical church, that common interest was the Christian religion (I'll not attempt to speak to the struggles of those who entered for marriage after falling in love with someone who is Orthodox, without a rigorous critical examination of comparative theology and historical scrutiny, as I have nothing of value to impart regarding that experience, though some things may nonetheless resonate with them. They rightly speak for themselves). As such, we tend to be less reflective of the Sunday entertainment or social club sectors of the Western Evangelical churches, but more the studious and religiously zealous types.

For those who have a significant depth of understanding regarding Orthodox spirituality and beliefs, the very foundations being radically distinct from those of our prior faith, many of us understand this to be in fact a completely different religion. Even shared theological terms have very different frameworks and meanings undergirding them. Sadly, though understandably, the common bond with some of those you love dearly will inevitably be broken. Not by an intentional shunning or deliberate severance, but by the loss of the common mind, the common beliefs, the common ethos once shared. These people are like family, and in some ways more than family, as family is not chosen and need not necessarily hold shared values on such deeply profound levels.

Suddenly you find you share little in those central aspects of your relationship. It's like you now speak a different language. And of course, where differences now arise, each believes the other errant, and this in what is seen by both as the most relevant matter of human existence. Separation is usually inevitable on some level. People can only talk about the weather for so long, and such people as these find mundane conversation rather uninteresting, which is a large part of what joined them together in the first place.

To now stand rather alone in an alien ethnic community with no real ties can be extremely isolating and lonely. And this by virtue of the choice to pursue truth, amid a people who almost exclusively were born into it and share a common ethnic background, who too seldom share that zeal. It's no wonder that many Americans who convert choose other Orthodox jurisdictions, with larger American convert populations, finding a greater sense of community. Yet on the other hand I believe there's a downside to the more familiar choice of a more convert-populated parish.

In my (admittedly limited) experience, many converts can tend to be Orthodox in their dogma and doctrine, yet remain Protestant in their ethos, in their thinking (frequently the *Sola scriptura* mindset is merely adjusted to a *Sola patristica* or canonically centered one, missing the heart and approach of the ancient faith). I truly believe submergence into an ethnic Orthodox congregation has some great benefits in this regard- the ethos and mindset are more absorbed than studied and learned. This is why my wife and I, even having many all-English "American" parishes (which are mostly Egyptian, though American born and/or raised) nearby, choose a much more ethnically Egyptian parish.

I cannot sufficiently stress the importance, and if this is only heard by a few people in any parish then that is sufficient, of bringing them into the social circles. Certainly, with the large and extended yet tight-knit Coptic family structure, it's easy not to notice the outsider in the congregation. But he often gave up by choice (personal relationships) what you take for granted in the religion of your birth, among friends you've known since childhood.

This is especially difficult at the time of the feasts. Being, as we are, on the Old Calendar, when we have finished the long and arduous season of fasting and preparation, there is no family with which to share this joyous event. Not even friends. This, the highlight of the communally shared season, is spent in seclusion. And even if you gathered the family to you after the liturgy at 1 AM, you didn't go through the fast together. You did not pray the festal liturgy together. They wouldn't even really understand what this really is all about, being only familiar with the scant remnants of the historical Christian feasts, now saturated in commercialism and relegated to perhaps some sermon and musical theme, for the one hour and fifteen-minute assembly Sunday morning.

From our Easter baptism until his departure to the East Coast for school, our Abouna Daniel had us in his home to join his family at Easter. I cannot express how much this meant to us and how great the sense of community embrace we felt. To this day he invites us over to visit with him and his family.

Since we came to our new parish, Abouna Joseph has also had us join his family at major feasts, instilling the same sense of belonging and love.

That any convert should not be invited to a Coptic family festal celebration in any parish is honestly shameful. Forgive me for that harshness, but it's true. If you are reading this, don't shake your head or merely feel sympathy—change it. It doesn't take a whole parish. It just takes you.

Syncretism

Allow me to begin here by saying that I get how this may well look like an overemphasis on this matter, and some may say I have an axe to grind. And there is some truth in that, but only some. While of course I feel cheated in some sense by having something so removed from the faith delivered by the Apostles taught to me as real Christianity, and while I admittedly look back on it as rather trite and superficial, I honestly believe my biggest motivation in this is fidelity.

Nothing could be more exemplary of traditions than the Orthodox Faith, properly understood and practiced. Traditions are something handed down, to be preserved intact, and handed down again. They are a baton in a relay race through the ages. This was a central theme in what God delivered to Moses at Sinai—to practice and preserve and pass down—and the charge given to those who received it. And to their children and all those after them. Preservation and practice without mixture with other religions was then and has been for two-thousand years of Orthodoxy more or less synonymous with faithfulness. When I chose to enter this tradition, in my mind then as now, was this same charge, inasmuch as I am able.

For ones who left a Western Evangelical church to enter Orthodoxy, to find the same songs sung at meetings, the same books on the shelf at the bookstore, and in rare cases (thank God!) the teachings mirrored or borrowed in an Orthodox parish, has an impact the cradle Orthodox can't quite appreciate. After all, we gave up deep and important personal relationships to be here. To find poor and out-of-place versions of what we thought we left behind in our pursuit of truth can be like a punch in the gut. It's not only the shallow self-help content and "Jesus is my boyfriend" music (again, a term I heard coined by more traditional Protestants), but the poor imitations of hip, cool, and funny preachers and youth pastors we abandoned in favor of the deeply wise and spiritual-minded amazing Coptic clergy. It's like going to see a Shakespeare play and finding the lead role played by an amateur comedian impersonating Jim Carrey. We didn't leave what we found to be errant, yet authentic in its innovation, in order to seek a poor knockoff of the errant.

Regarding issues of theology or living the spiritual life itself, I find virtually nothing from the Protestant West needing to be appropriated, as anything true would be known to be true only by comparison to what was handed down in the Apostolic churches for two millennia. And if you already have an accurate tape measure, what is the value in obtaining a stick with measurement markings and seeking to determine which marks are correct and useful by comparing it to your tape measure? Why not just use your tape measure in the first place?

I think it worth noting here that while I attend a parish which prays and chants in Coptic, English, and Arabic, I believe all-English parishes are important alternatives. One ought to pray with the understanding, as Saint Paul teaches. Yet a few things, easily learned and understood, like the Trisagion hymn, the *Doxa Patri* and *Ke nin* responses, etc. are much welcomed by many of us as ties to the continuity of the ancient faith. I can say that for me, knowing I'm joining the Ancients in the same exact phraseology is grounding and deeply important. I see the goal as accessibility as well as joining in the unbroken continuity of the ancient faith, while removing unnecessary obstacles, not the eradication of a different language. And certainly not bringing in the Asherah poles from the religion of the neighbors.

I do try to be mindful of the good intents behind what I think they think are cultural adaptations. Whether by an attempt to attract more numbers, or to keep the younger Copts from leaving, or from sympathy for the outsider who feels alienated as discussed above, or by a desire to simply ethnically adapt to Americanism, the intention is benevolent. At least I presume so. Or hope so. While I think I somewhat understand the problems associated with the cultural barriers facing the visitor to a Coptic parish, having been one many times, which can at times come off as unwelcoming and suspicious, as well as those experienced in being the child of an immigrant in a new land, which I was, I also understand that one must be acutely aware of what is religious and what is cultural in order to address things. And of course, one must be mindful of one's own bias as established by one's own experiences.

I think I understand the backlash against the elder Copts, who may at times errantly believe every aspect of their practices and beliefs to be dogma/doctrine, to be held tightly and passed on without alteration. Sadly, as may well be the case sometimes, no distinction is made between the cultural and theological, understandably. They themselves have come from a place with the more pressing matters of survival and fidelity to the faith taking precedence over carefully parsing out the theological from the cultural in a land where the distinction isn't really too relevant for all intents and purposes anyway.

I would hope younger Copts could come to appreciate the value of their elders' fidelity and yes, even their unyielding stubbornness(!) as an integral part of why they (the younger) were even born into a Christian home in the first place. Remember that this is the small remnant who held the faith against all odds and pressures. A little understanding and appreciation for the good possessed by these elders may help curtail the tendency to overreact. Their incentives to abandon this faith were surely greater than any the younger ones will face here in America, yet they never did. In understanding one's own frustrations I hope one could also understand the likelihood of that pendulum being swung too far the other way in reaction, and be watchful for it.

However, seeing these various problems, it also seems pretty clear to me that those frequently proposing and implementing the solutions are simply in no position to adequately do so, having willingness and popularity as the primary reasons for being in leadership roles (much respect given here from me for their tireless and well-intended efforts in their service). I have no idea how, but somewhere along the line in American culture we've come to believe that merely seeing a problem qualifies one to assess the scope and implement the best solutions.

Not being theologically astute regarding their own faith, having memorized ritual and hymns but not understanding the meanings, lacking awareness of how the things they inherited came to be, and most of all having no understanding whatsoever of the theology and ethos undergirding the Protestant importations, they are simply ill equipped, though well intentioned, for such a task. Copying the Evangelicals won't do the trick. Not only are the copies very poor quality (and why take a poor imitation when you can have the authentic?), but the Evangelicals are hemorrhaging members as theirs is a lackluster imitation of what the world has anyway. To quote Hank Hill, commenting on the authentic version of contemporary Christian music, "Can't you tell you're not making Christianity any better, you're just making Rock & Roll worse."

While I again believe I understand and even sympathize with some who, in their desire to make things better, import from the neighboring religions into their parishes, the result is no less damaging, and requires correction.

This correction ought to begin with a removal of that which is not born of our faith. Then we must obtain a true understanding of what is in front of us on both counts (Orthodoxy and Evangelical religion/culture) before acting. Only by first grasping the meaning, reasons, and ethos of the things we inherited can we begin to understand the importance as well as the proper distinction between the religious and the cultural. Indeed, the cultural is generally a form which bears the substance of something theological, as most cultures have deeply religious histories, and too often can one seek to adapt to the cultural form and inadvertently import a different substance. This is certainly a likely result when one lacks understanding of Western religions from which Western culture is largely formed and/or influenced. There must be a well-informed scrutiny of the things we wish to import. One must properly grasp the history, theology, and ethos of what one finds appealing in order to determine if it fits.

As an example, being somewhat well-read in the area of apologetics, and being taught Orthodoxy by a very deeply Orthodox priest, together with having spent decades in Protestantism, I believe myself to be fairly capable of consuming Western apologetics materials while also catching and removing any theological bents or errors, as a dear friend says, "eating the watermelon and spitting out the seeds." I am always reluctant to direct any cradle Copts towards these materials, even though they are at the forefront of the important field of apologetics, because they seldom understand either faith in such manner as would be crucial in preventing the import of errors.

While I see and even agree with the problematic nature of some of the issues which have prompted these importations, I simply believe the proposed and implemented resolutions will do more harm than good in the long run, not to mention God's response historically to those who turned to neighboring religions to supplement what they considered lacking in what He gave them. That has never gone well.

While some tweaking may well be in order in some ways, before we do that, we need to first understand, appreciate, and teach why we do what we do. For instance, the simple chest pat used to greet or display acceptance or acquiescence is lovely, even if not doctrinal and of cultural and thus non-essential origins. Simply understanding it reveals its beauty.

Then we can discuss, with historians and theologians and former Protestants who were astute in their former religion, what adjustments to make in America. Why we are not frequently consulting other Orthodox jurisdictions who have had great success with converts, while keeping their Orthodoxy Orthodox, is beyond me. We do not need to reinvent the wheel. Responses from friends in Eastern Orthodox jurisdictions who also converted from Protestant backgrounds, when I tell them of the Evangelical importations, tend to be "WHAT??? Are you kidding? If you're going to copy the Protestants, why copy the ones that knowledgeable Protestants mock?"

Finally, I'd like to challenge the presumption that a lack of appeal or outright rejection of this faith necessarily speaks to some flaw which needs fixing. Whether the masses who screamed "Crucify Him!", or the "Stumbling block to the Jews" or "Foolishness to the Gentiles" (I Corinthians 1:23), this religion is centered around a cross, an implement of death, calling adherents to follow in self-sacrifice. It is not merely counter-cultural, but calls one to go against all known self-interest.

I think in many cases this move to make things more fun, appealing, and popular is rooted in a flawed American assumption of better marketing and trend following as the solution to poor sales. When you're selling self-denial and a cross, why be surprised to find it hard to obtain and retain customers?

No, I think in most cases we don't have a marketing problem here, but rather a product problem. And the use of a "bait-and-switch" tactic, offering something fun and immediately fulfilling, is not only disingenuous, but can misdirect those within the church who truly are seeking the ancient and authentic faith we hold towards an unfulfilling (in the long run) pseudo-spirituality. Back in our time serving among Evangelicals, my wife and I noticed that as this user-friendly fun version of Protestantism was implemented more and more, the would-be true disciples had less and less into which they could invest their zeal. Sure, they attracted larger numbers, but those seeking something more profound and substantial soon left for a more sober and zealous group in some other church.

Many years ago, Anastasia came across a photo and article criticizing the way our livestock were pumped up with hormones. The photo showed huge animals who had to be rolled down the ramp from the truck because they couldn't even walk. She likened this to what was happening in our Evangelical churches, being pumped full of substances to make them larger, but being very unhealthy.

Larger does *not* mean better.

Again, these issues require careful parsing to determine which issues have which root, which things are cultural and which religious, and are not the sort of thing best handled by those whose sole qualifications are zeal, popularity, and compassion. Such things require careful and intelligent thought, knowledge and guidance.

Cultural Differences

This area gets dicey. But before delving into tensions, I hope to provide some balancing context. I hope the reader keeps in mind that I choose to be here in the Coptic Orthodox Church. While virtually every Orthodox jurisdiction is available to me within a short driving distance here in Southern California, this is the one I chose and continue to choose. I absolutely LOVE Egyptian people, with their warmth, cultural moral propriety (to which I often fail to live up), their love for the Faith, their simple and humble trust in God, and their amazing sense of humor. I even find their disorganization (which was at first a challenge to this German raised American) charming (provided I just sit back and watch, uninvolved). There are aspects of the warm emotionalism which are strongly reminiscent of the Mexican culture of my childhood and life in Southern California.

I am here by choice, having no familial connections to bind me. And as explained above, their spirituality is something I consider essential for my own growth. Please read the following with this in mind.

Also be aware that these are matters of personal experience and subjective observations. While they may resonate with some, particularly traditionally-oriented Americans, others may not find them problematic and may have different tensions in their own experience. This is not intended to be comprehensive.

From time to time, a Protestant inquirer is directed to me for assistance, due primarily to my being theologically bilingual (Protestant and Orthodox) and having a fairly decent grasp of both systems of thought. At some point, usually early on, I explain the jurisdictional options as I have come to experience them.

Heavily ethnic (primarily immigrant population) parishes possess the deepest form of the Coptic ethos, but there is a cultural barrier that not everyone can penetrate, and for those who can it takes a long time. Rarely are older Egyptian immigrants warm and welcoming to outsiders. Again, this is not a criticism. It is rooted in a fear of *other* which has an understandable basis. From the history of oppression and persecution to the coming of European missionaries, the outsider has never been very supportive, to put it mildly.

Coptic "American" parishes tend to be most warm and welcoming, being primarily American born and/or raised, but do not possess the ethos in the same way their elders do. Again, understandably. I am convinced that only living under persecution and real discrimination can one have such things formed in this way. This is not to say that the American born/raised Copts do not have other, at least equally important attributes in excess of the immigrant communities. None is better in my view, so much as it is simply different. Having said that, I have seen in some a misguided, yet well-intentioned attempt at cultural assimilation result in importing Protestant ideas, materials and ethos, as described above. So, there can be quite a variance parish to parish. I've seen a few wonderful examples which are warm and welcoming, all-English, and fully Orthodox, not importing from Evangelicalism, and unashamedly Coptic. The main warning I offer to inquirers who are considering an American Coptic parish is that of the possibility of relocation. What if you move one day and there is only an ethnic parish nearby? What then? Can you still thrive spiritually?

Then I explain the option of some other jurisdictions, inhabited by more Americans, usually converts. Here they will be right at home, relate to people, find the theological knowledge they seek, and be surrounded by those who share their zeal. Yet, the ethos is, once again, not the same, and understandably so. Most people with whom I have spent considerable time (when I meet with an inquirer to answer questions and discuss these matters, commonly in multiple four-hour sessions) who ultimately convert end up in the Antiochian Church.

I think it extremely important here to gain some perspective when discussing jurisdictional options.

Believing we possess something wonderful, we ought to want to share it with others, and that is good. On the other hand, becoming salesmen of our product, seeking the sales commission of affirmation by our community peers, which follows the

American consumerist church model, in which there is a church on every corner competing for customers, constantly needing to up the game to beat out the competition, is *not* Orthodox!

What is the goal? Is it adding a new convert feather to our caps? Is it a new tithe giver to help support our parish? Is it to display how connected and relevant we are to the culture around us? Is it to be more American and less Egyptian? Some honest introspection is needed here to truly ascertain the motives of our own hearts, which will likely show a mixture of motives, and not a clean and pure singularity.

Ought the Orthodox goal not be to take a lost and suffering person and connect them to God to begin a lifelong process of spiritual healing and growth? If so, then truly it would result in our willingness to invest ourselves with no expectation of personal return, individually, or as a parish, or as a jurisdiction. If this growth seems best facilitated by some other jurisdiction for that individual, then we should gladly see them depart at some point, rejoicing that they are growing in Christ.

Next on the list of cultural difficulties, and the hardest for me over the years, have been two closely related issues: appearance over integrity and pacification over resolution.

A very knowledgeable friend, a Coptic therapist, recently thumbnailed the differences between our American culture, which is highly individualistic, in which what we know of ourselves is paramount, even to the point of looking down on those to whom approval of others is valued, and that of the Egyptians (as well as many other cultures), for whom community and upholding one's status in it takes a prominent role. In short, the difference between personal integrity and appearance to others in the community, the vertical and the horizontal orientations.

As you read the following, keep in mind that what I'm hoping to convey is that each culture has pros and cons, extremes which are not healthy, and emphases that are understood by each respective culture, and off-putting to the other. I'm merely expressing tensions, not thinking I have any perfect resolutions, beyond perhaps some awareness of each other's backgrounds, a bit of understanding and allowance, and perhaps a move towards the middle for those of us who tend too far into our respective directions.

The traditional American ethos, whether through literature, movies, television, or other means, has often portrayed the man who stood alone, wrongly accused or believed of being cowardly or guilty of breaking some common moral code, who did what he knew was right, not caring to defend himself against his accusers or critics, nor caring about their opinions, only to be found right and noble at the end, sending a message of condemnation to those who judge wrongly, and affirmation to those who stand alone for what is right, to their respective audiences. Fierce individualism is in our blood. Sadly, a sense of community is largely absent when this goes to extremes.

Truly the concepts found deep in the Orthodox theological ethos like, "I am not saved until my brother is saved" and, "we fall alone, but are only saved together" would send a shudder down the spine of many American Christians when not understood in context.

Yet that which is beneficial in sharing community, that which can be rightly utilized in keeping a brother from falling by keeping some personal failures private, not enticing others by displaying our sin, community pressures which can help to curtail immoral behavior, can lead to its own downsides. Namely, a lack of personal integrity. When appearance to the community is what matters most, hypocrisy is inevitable. We can and do lose sight of the fact of a life lived in the presence of God, never being beyond His view, in which one lives looking upwards at Him and inward at self in careful examination. Rather, we may fix our gaze horizontally, at others, seeing our identity and value in what they perceive. Few things more repugnant to a moral, traditional American than hypocrisy and fake piety.

An American friend told me of one of the most painful experiences of his Coptic life which I believe will be helpful in understanding the perspective of one from our culture. He too was a convert, full of zeal.

It seems he had said some things on social media about a popular church figure which were controversial insofar as they criticized a clergyman, yet nobody had presented any substantive complaint regarding the accuracy of his criticisms. And the popular figure certainly had not seen any need to change, despite prior, much less public criticisms. Soon thereafter, he posted a (completely unrelated, the only real context being the two at an event) a photo of himself with a clergyman whom he loved dearly and considered a father (*Abouna*, *Anba*, and *Baba*, terms for priests, bishops and the Pope are all indeed derived from "father"). He told me of his love for this clergyman, and how he would smile and have a deep sense of warmth whenever he saw him. He truly felt as if he mattered to this man, a sense of being loved.

The clergyman asked him to remove the picture of the two of them because, "people might think I approve of the things you said." The man was crushed.

You see, while I am sure this clergyman had a good intent regarding his image in the sight of the people, and avoidance of controversy, what he conveyed to this man was, "I can't be seen with you because of what someone *might* errantly think." The man conveyed to me how he literally wept, having a sense of deep and painful abandonment, of being disowned as a son, for the sake of appearance. The scars left behind remained long after he decided, "Well, he's not my father, but my clergyman. Our relationship is relegated to that of ecclesial roles."

Rather than correct any clearly contrived and wrong inferences someone may draw from the picture, the clergyman chose to distance himself from my friend for the sake of possible appearances.

Similarly, the issue of what constitutes the resolution of an issue can be problematic. For those charged with keeping the peace and facilitating the salvation of all church members, maintaining the appearance of impartiality and seeking harmony can easily result in a mindset in which "nobody talking about the problem" is considered resolution.

While we Americans may have a tendency to pick at a wound incessantly, not allowing it to heal, in the ditch on the other side of the road can lie a tendency to cover over a wound without first cleaning it out thoroughly, sometimes neglecting required surgery so to speak, leading to a harmful infection that is yet unseen in the present moment. The reluctance to insist on final moral categories and accountability regarding what was done by the parties, in an attempt to not alienate the offender, can prolong, perhaps indefinitely, the circumstances and dispositions which cause a wound to fester. Again, conversely, in American culture when we see a problem we often tend to rush in, guns blazing, and exacerbate it, when leaving it alone would have perhaps allowed it to heal on its own. I suppose in these matters there is a huge need for wisdom and also a willingness to apply the appropriate response.

My intent here is to explain the point of view from one in my own ditch. Coptic dispositions to problems can be seen as highly unjust. "Sweeping things under the rug" when someone has been wronged is another one of those American taboos.

Lastly, and I won't expound on the cultural reasons I've been told (which help in understanding "how," but don't speak to a Christian "ought"), but rather rely on the core ethos of Orthodox Christianity as the proper standard, there is the issue of addressing personal offense.

It was shocking for me to learn of long-time feuds between people and families. Both the inability to admit fault and the inability to forgive an offense had me bewildered for some time, and to some extent still does. I mean, both issues, repentance and forgiveness, could not be more central in our religion, regardless of expression. From the Lord Himself, to the saints on the walls, to the readings and homilies, I'd be hard-pressed to find a more prominent theme. Yet here we are with the Hatfields and McCoys coming up for communion after the kiss of peace. Are they even aware we are not to take communion when we hold an unresolved grudge against another? So strange.

Chapter 25

Assorted Observations

Evangelism is largely lacking in the Coptic world, on the individual level. I am shocked to find that so few younger Copts speak of their faith to the world they encounter. While understandable in Egypt, where you're either already a Copt or else certainly aware of who they are, and where active evangelism could well cost one dearly, there is little excuse here in America for turning a blind eye to a hurting world around you which needs Christ simply because you don't want to feel uncomfortable or cause discomfort in others. On the other hand, having too few culturally accessible parishes, largely lacking a true understanding of the meanings of the faith and practices they possess, and also having at times religious syncretism with Western Evangelicalism in the more accessible all-English parishes, perhaps this is best until we can sort out and obtain some better uniformity of belief and practice. I suppose this has left me where I am, being involved in evangelism to some extent, yet most often directing the inquirer at some point to another jurisdiction. For now.

Egyptians will be late. They know it and joke about it. You won't change that. Get over it. Plan accordingly. Don't put yourself in a position where tardiness will be offensive or problematic to you.

Older Egyptians will be stubborn. Don't try to brow beat them into changing. It won't work. Keep in mind that this stubbornness is an important part of why this church even exists, against all odds. Work around it. See the tremendous good in them and what they can pass down to you. If you're a younger American-born Egyptian, you do not need to change a parish in order to offer a more welcoming experience to outsiders nearly as much as you simply need to be that welcoming person. Help the visitor, take him to lunch, and answer his questions. Include him in your immediate social group. That is sufficient. Also, explain the persecuted history of the elders and why they are suspicious of the "other." If you are the visitor and so "woke" in your modern Americanism that you've become what a friend once called an "inveterate offense collector," then this simply isn't for you. Even should you find that one amazing parish where no elder Egyptians look at you with a critical and suspicious expression, which is unthinkable in the Evangelical user-friendly churches, you'll no doubt run into it sooner or later. If your skin is very thin, some other jurisdictional alternative is a better fit. No harm, no foul; simply a mismatch.

Egyptians have a wonderful sense of humor, the best of any ethnic group I have encountered. Often self-deprecating, if you're too "woke," you may find yourself totally confused if you're supposed to be outraged at the racism of someone laughing about another culture, or if that would be racist because the one joking is of that culture himself. Quite the quandary. If you love humor, enjoy it. You'll find no shortage here.

Copts, whose upbringing in the church teaches the rigid morals, delayed gratification, emphasis on education, and self-discipline, which together translate into great career success when applied in the generally unencumbered West, too often neglect the primacy of the spiritual life and obtaining salvation itself. Salvation, as noted above, can be taken for granted as members of the community and partakers of the sacraments.

Wealth and materialistic pursuits, alongside the prestige of careers, which especially include titles, can be dangerous traps. Mindfulness of the teachings of the historical Church regarding humility, austerity and modesty, generosity and spiritual centeredness, are essential in combatting the perils of the worldly success which is common.

The issue of use of the Coptic language in the liturgy is complex, and I don't believe has a simple answer. It's not a matter of right and wrong, but rather one of competing "good" things, in my opinion. Understanding what we are praying is a good thing, obviously. But so is carrying on a cultural legacy which is marked by sacrifice, martyrdom, and a rich history of desert spirituality. While the language is cultural, not religious per se (please, the whole leg crossing in church thing. I'm pretty sure that's cultural, so maybe ease up a bit on your strict enforcement?!), that doesn't make it automatically something needing to be jettisoned. Preserving something which bears these historical realities is understandable and commendable. With these competing factors, I believe the best course is the one we are on: allowing each parish to choose what languages, or mixtures of languages and in what proportions, best suit the local congregation.

Being from a history of persecution, the ethos of most clergy is one of comfort and encouragement. Naturally. Therefore, there is a reluctance to offer a swift boot to the pants when needed much of the time. The balanced approach of which Abouna Daniel spoke, "a priest's job is to comfort the afflicted and afflict the comforted" isn't too common. As a result, people can have a presumption of spiritual safety through observation of some rules and rituals, when perhaps some of the time there ought to be more of a sense of peril. This always strikes me as similar to the Jews, whose claims, "We have Abraham as our father" (we have a hereditary right to salvation) and, "We observe the law" (we follow the rules and rituals) were met by warnings from Christ to attend to matters of the heart and personal daily devotion to the things of God. So, to the convert I would say, "Know yourself first. If you're highly self-critical and tend to be too hard on yourself, the priest who comforts and encourages will be easy to find. But if you need one who challenges and pushes you, that may take a little searching."

After two thousand years of attending to persecuted sheep, I believe the Coptic clergy to be the best priests on the planet. Yes, I'm heavily biased. Their care and sympathy, their love for the people, their accessible guidance and tireless devotion to the people of their parishes give me confidence that I could go anywhere in the world that the Coptic Church exists and continue my spiritual path as effectively as my willingness to listen and obey enables. To the convert I would say if at some point you become frustrated with some of the people, or even hierarchy and some of their decisions, or God forbid some scandal, it is ultimately your own Father of Confession who will get you to heaven. This is where your Orthodox life is truly lived out, under his personal guidance. Take your eyes off the distractions when they become disruptive to your spiritual progress and run back to Abouna and the liturgy.

Beyond this, one spiritual mentor, usually a godparent, ought to be a second, complimentary voice guiding your journey.

Lastly, while I appreciate that in the Coptic Church the clergy (especially Bishops and the Pope) are the rock stars, in contrast to my Evangelical past in which the rock stars are actual rock stars, this can be taken a bit too far. The pushing and struggling to touch the visiting bishop or Pope and take his blessing, the throngs of people, some of whom seldom otherwise come to church, can be a little bit out of control. I heard a story of a grandmother actually biting a large deacon in the side who was providing crowd control to get him to move so she could reach our Pope and "take his blessing." Maybe we ought to consider our strolling in late and having such a casual attitude by comparison when it is "just Jesus Christ Himself" who is literally present on the altar?

Chapter 26

*"Entreat me not to leave you,
Or to turn back from following after you;
For wherever you go, I will go;
And wherever you lodge, I will lodge;
Your people shall be my people,
And your God, my God."
Ruth 1: 16-17*

When I asked of some friends on social media, "What questions would you have for a study-in convert to the Coptic Church?" one stood out above the others: "Why do you stay?"

Admittedly, there are some culture clashes which can at times leave me quite frustrated. There are some serious issues of syncretism with Evangelical Protestantism, mentioned above, which absolutely hit a very sensitive area for one who has come from the world they are trying to mimic (and poorly at that), invoking the obvious self-questioning, "Did you really come here for a cheesy copy of what you left?" This becomes even more taxing when I speak to Orthodox converts in other jurisdictions whose response is to be appalled and an assurance that nothing even close to this would be permitted in their jurisdictions. Of course, the temptation to change jurisdictions crosses one's mind, especially in the absence of ethnic and familial ties which keep those around you from such considerations. Fortunately, this issue occurs at the parish level only, enabling one to simply look the other way when he has found a very traditionally Coptic parish as I have. Unfortunately, looking the other way is antithetical to the ethos of an American.

For better and worse, the Coptic Church tends to be more organic and less uniform. Not being an imperial church, the need for uniformity from place to place is historically less important. For better, as it allows the flexibility at the diocese and more so parish levels to adjust and accommodate the local needs. For worse, as it allows local errors or problems to go unaddressed. Similarly, the gentle and patient demeanor of many hierarchs can foster a warm and loving environment of belonging, or an unchecked divergence into problems which grow over time, causing substantial damage, before finally (if ever) being resolved.

I speak only for me here, but the chant style just does not resonate. A few hymns do, but mostly not. My ear is hopelessly Western, and Latin as well as Russian and other styles are much more appealing. Sorry, but I just didn't grow up with this, and it's not only very much "other," but I can't learn it at my age with my mental elasticity diminishing.

So why stay?

First and foremost, I need to be saved. I am a mess and I know it. As noted earlier, the Copts possess in abundance the characteristics I lack most. While I have no interest in becoming Egyptian, as I remind Coptic friends sometimes, I do desire to become more Orthodox. And of the various Orthodox attributes and cultural offerings, theirs seem to best suit my spiritual needs.

Back when I was inquiring into Orthodoxy, the primary scholarly resources I found seemed to be Greek and Russian. Florovsky was indeed a treasure. But it occurred to me that I could obtain these wonderful works by ordering a book. The ethos by which I needed to be surrounded and immersed couldn't be found on Amazon. I had to drive to a parish and sit down in it. In fact, knowing my background, story and knowledge obtained prior to baptism would be somewhat unique among the local Coptic community, Abouna Daniel in his wisdom (I'm not kidding. At thirty-three years old he had the wisdom of a man at least twice that age) told me just to sit down for some time in a pew and do nothing. I'm grateful to this day that he did.

This work of change is dreadfully slow, no longer seeing growth time in days or weeks but years and decades, and I often feel as if I'm just beginning, or else making no progress at all (which I understand to be common among those undertaking this journey of Orthodox spiritual development).

Thankfully, from my parish priests where I pray to visiting a few local parishes from time to time, (as I love the priests and congregations), in fact almost all Coptic priests I encounter, and the wonderful parish friends at my home parish, and a few other close Coptic friends, this has truly become a home for my wife and I.

While there have been impasses which had me seriously considering leaving, seeing various attributes which resonate more strongly with me in other jurisdictions, especially in the area of keeping Protestantism properly defined as "a different religion" since they have much greater theological knowledge in this area, such impulses always seem to follow my exposure and attention to things outside my parish, or even diocese. The solution seems to be in returning to my home parish for the small, quiet Friday liturgy with Abouna Andrew and my friend Mike, taking my eyes off the problem and getting them back on Christ, and my own salvation.

I can anticipate the criticisms of this solution by many zealous Orthodox who read this and see me as advocating for burying my head in the sand, and only plead for mercy. To them I say that my disposition and goal must remain first and foremost aligned with the one Abouna Daniel had once stated was his own concerning me (at the time I was in tears and broken over his guidance on some issue): "I don't care if you're not happy. My goal is to get you (points at me) there (points upward) when this is all over."

About the Authors

Thilo Young is a lover of reason, theology, and God. These three loves have led him into numerous roles during his lifetime—serving as a lead coordinator at a mega-church, leading comprehensive theology teachings with young people and eventually, to the doors of the Coptic Orthodox Church. His deep understanding of the Christian faith has been refined over decades of examination and testing. He has debated passionate atheists, challenged PhD theologians, and learned at the feet of priests. His great love also extends to the Coptic Church herself as seen in his well-received article, "An American Viewpoint of an Egyptian Mother."

Anastasia Young is a Director of Communications at a worldwide apologetics ministry, where she has been employed for 18 years. In addition to her formal occupation, Anastasia serves alongside Thilo in offering people of all ages, a defense for the Christian faith.

Thilo and Anastasia live in Southern California and have enjoyed nearly 20 years of marriage surrounded by their loving family, friends, and their delightful granddaughter.

www.ingramcontent.com/pod-product-compliance
Lightning Source LLC
Chambersburg PA
CBHW030520080526
44586CB00011B/264